A Melody of Hope

A Melody of Hope

Surviving Your Daughter's Eating Disorder

CATHY ROBINSON

iUniverse, Inc.
Bloomington

A Melody of Hope
Surviving Your Daughter's Eating Disorder

iUniverse books may be ordered through booksellers or by contacting:

iUniverse
1663 Liberty Drive
Bloomington, IN 47403
www.iuniverse.com
1-800-Authors (1-800-288-4677)

ISBN: 978-1-4620-1190-2 (pbk)
ISBN: 978-1-4620-1192-6 (clth)
ISBN: 978-1-4620-1191-9 (ebk)

Printed in the United States of America

iUniverse rev. date: 07/20/2011

For my daughter Melody

I am humbled by the courage and strength you had to recover from your eating disorder. You are my hero.

To my daughters who suffered emotionally while our home was in chaos, I thank God that He carried you in His arms and helped you heal.

Love you forever, my precious girls.

Acknowledgments

To my dear friend and colleague Barb Pesut, thank you for taking the time from your incredibly busy schedule to edit parts of this book. I am forever grateful for your expertise and advice.

To Danielle Robinson, your master's degree in sociology was immensely beneficial in preparing and editing this book. Bless you, my darling and brilliant daughter.

CONTENTS

The Lord hears his people when they call to him for help.
He rescues them from all their troubles.

—Psalms 34:17

Foreword

Ten years ago, our then thirteen-year-old daughter, Denise, suffered from anorexia nervosa. When I first heard about Cathy Robinson's book and her invitation for mothers of daughters with eating disorders to write their stories, I was eager to contribute my own narrative. Many times during the worst of our family's struggles, I wished there had been just such a book, a chronicle of hope. I longed for some glimpse of assurance that we would get through the suffering intact, that the dark would be replaced by light, and that we could return to some kind of normalcy. During the most difficult times of her illness, I remember bargaining with God: *I will endure this anguish if you just let me know somehow that she is going to be okay.*

At first, it seemed that writing my story would be an easy task, for after all, had I not written and rewritten the story in my mind for years? Did I not remember every step of this long and at times arduous journey? I prided myself on having grown through the experience from initially wanting to deny and hide the pain, to seeking support from family, friends, and health care professionals, to finally speaking quite openly about our daughter's struggles with anorexia in a wider community where I work as a nursing instructor. I believed that after all we had been through, I was beyond stigmatizing those who grapple with mental illness by hiding our own reality. Writing my story seemed a positive way to not only benefit personally from the cathartic release of energy tied to these experiences, but also to encourage others in their journey of healing.

To my surprise, I was not as evolved as I thought. It was difficult to see the words on paper, to sort through the myriad of emotions and events, to relive aspects of the experiences, questioning why things happened as they did. I worried that in expressing my struggles, my daughter might be traumatized all over again by the knowledge that her illness had a profound impact on her mother. What right did I have to decide that the private pains of my family members should be published for others to read? All these and other thoughts hindered my attempts to write the story. I procrastinated past the deadline for submission, pacifying myself with the idea that it just was not all that important for others to read my story.

When Denise came home from university for a visit in the summer, she asked me how the story was coming along. I shared my reticence openly with her. She listened intently to all my worries with no apparent judgments. But then she offered, "Mom, maybe the story is about how hard it is to write the story. Maybe others need to hear that part too."

So I wrote my story. The words came easily, and there was a sense of triumph in realizing how far we have come. I shared it first with Denise and the rest of our family, for after all, it is their story too. I am happy to share it with any other mother who may also be longing for hope and searching for light in the darkness of eating disorders.

Ruth Dubois

Jesus looked at them intently and said,
"Humanly speaking, it is impossible. But with God
everything is possible."

—Matthew 19:26

Introduction

Our journey began in 2005, when I first discovered Melody's eating disorder. Life spiraled downhill for our whole family over the ensuing year, and I wondered how we would survive it. I was a single mom with four daughters. After my husband passed away, I had to work extra hours to bring in enough money to pay the bills. I felt guilty, as I was too busy working to spend much time with my girls. Melody seemed more affected by my absence than the others, but I missed her cues. I found out much later that she was suffering with an anxiety disorder, and she worried constantly that I might die.

As Melody approached her high school graduation, she became moody and withdrawn. I noticed some weight loss but thought she was just a little anxious about graduation. It wasn't until she had lost a significant amount of weight that I started paying attention. I kept telling myself that she would be okay and that this was just temporary. Instead, she continued to lose weight; and one fateful day in April 2005, I heard her purging and knew I had to deal with it. I did not want to tell anyone, as I felt guilty and thought that somehow I had caused this and was a terrible mother. I tried to help Melody by controlling what she ate and did every day. After all, I was a pediatric nurse and convinced myself that I could handle it without telling anyone. This was a costly mistake, as my daughter continued to deteriorate until she nearly died.

I remember attending a support group for families of children with eating disorders with the hope of receiving encouragement.

Unfortunately, the room was filled with parents struggling to deal with the pain, family chaos, and helplessness they felt. Although it was beneficial to be with others who understood my pain and fear, I so badly wanted to hear from families with a daughter who had recovered so that I could draw from their encouraging words and support. I decided I was more disheartened after attending the meetings and therefore stopped going. I felt more alone, hopeless, guilty, and terrified than I had ever felt in my life. Finally, in desperation, I reached out for help from doctors, counselors, friends, and a treatment facility for Melody; and with hard work, she slowly but surely recovered, and our family healed.

After Melody recovered, I decided to write about my journey as the mother of a daughter with an eating disorder and what I learned. It was one of the hardest things I have ever done. While writing about our experience, I would cry so hard that I had to stop and walk away. Remembering brought the pain and anguish of Melody's suffering back to the present, and I couldn't bear it. I persevered, and when my story was finished, I had an amazing sense of peace and closure. I had healed. I also realized my story had a positive ending with my daughter fully recovered and our family healed. I thought how reading a story like that would have given me the hope and encouragement I needed to support my daughter through her struggle. This knowledge birthed the idea of offering a collection of true inspirational stories written by mothers to provide the much-needed encouragement, hope, and support to other mothers beginning their painful family journey. After putting out the call for submissions, I was blessed beyond measure reading the stories that came in. I understood the pain of reliving the experience of having a child with an eating disorder. I know there is a tendency to want to bury the past and never talk about it again because even though we survived, the pain, fear, and guilt live on in our minds when we don't achieve emotional healing and closure. The fear that the eating disorder could rear its ugly head again lurks in the recesses of our mind, so we dare not speak of it. But I also know speaking about our experience and sharing our pain can bring the ultimate healing and closure we need. That is what these brave mothers did;

they began talking and writing and healing. I am humbled by their honesty and courage; and I pray that this book will be a blessing to you and that you will find encouragement, hope, and support in knowing that your daughter can recover and live the life God destined her to live.

I also tell you this: If two of you agree here on earth concerning anything you ask, my Father in heaven will do it for you.

—**Matthew 18:19**

Chapter One

Slipping through My Fingers

Cathy Robinson

It was September 2009, and I was sitting in a chair outside the change room of the bridal shop. Melody was trying on wedding dresses for her upcoming wedding. While I anxiously waited to see her first selection, Melody's bridesmaids were chatting excitedly about the piles of dresses she would try on. I was suddenly overwhelmed with joy and gratitude, as there was a time when I could never have imagined this scene. Melody suffered an eating disorder that nearly took her life. I struggled to understand her pain but simply could not. Our family rode a turbulent roller coaster, and we wondered if we could survive this living hell. As I watched my daughter slowly slipping away, I found solace in a song written by ABBA.

Slipping through My Fingers

Do I really see what's in her mind
Each time I think I'm close to knowing
She keeps on growing
Slipping through my fingers all the time.

While humming the song in my head, I heard Melody announce she was ready to show her first dress. When the curtain opened, I

1

gasped, and tears immediately sprang into my eyes. She was beautiful and filled out the dress to perfection. There was no evidence of her former disease—she was healthy and glowing. "Praise the Lord," was all I could muster at that moment. I heard the ooohs and ahhhs from her bridal party and watched as Melody lapped up all the love. This was going to be a wonderful day! When she slipped into the dressing room to try on another dress, I couldn't help but think back to the time when the eating disorder reared its ugly head and nearly killed my precious daughter.

*   *   *

It was April 2005, and I was sitting in my home office. I could hear Melody downstairs through the heating vent—she was vomiting. I had heard her several times over the past few weeks. It was always the same pattern:

1. Huge meal consumed quickly
2. Hurried exit from kitchen
3. Bathroom door closes
4. Water running in the sink
5. Emerges red eyed and flushed

In the beginning, I pushed the thought of an eating disorder far from my mind. I thought, *This is not happening to my daughter! . . . This is not happening to our family! . . . I am just imagining this . . . She looks well . . . She is not overly thin . . . She seems happy . . .*

I sat staring at the heating vent and listening, but my heart was pounding so loudly that I couldn't hear anything. I could feel my breathing getting faster . . . and a lump formed in my throat . . . I couldn't swallow . . . my mouth was suddenly very dry . . . my hands were shaking . . . I didn't want to hear this . . . I wanted to run downstairs and tell her to stop it . . . but I didn't . . . I couldn't face it or her or this horrible reality . . . instead, I just sat and listened and fought back tears.

I heard myself murmur, "Please, God, make her stop this. Heal her body and mind. Help her love herself." I rambled on and on in my head . . . I didn't know what I was saying or if it made sense. I did know that this disease kills young women, and now it has attacked my daughter. Oh God no!

I felt alone and terrified and powerless . . . I remember praying, *God, please take care of this. I can't do it alone.*

*   *   *

My mind came back to the present as Melody emerged to reveal another wedding dress. More ooohs and ahhhs . . . it was hard to believe that she was even more beautiful in this gown. I couldn't contain myself and jumped up to hug her. Her bridesmaids were gushing and declared that this was the "one," but Melody was having too much fun to stop. There was a row of gowns, and she was determined to try them all on. She headed into the dressing room, and again, my mind wandered back in time—this time, to Melody's birth in 1987.

*   *   *

She was a beautiful, quiet tiny baby. I loved holding her. With blonde hair and blue eyes, she looked just like her older sisters. As a toddler, she was very shy and quiet and clung to me when we went out. She did not seem to adjust well when her younger sister was born and constantly competed for my attention.

When my husband passed away in 1996, I was left with four children. My daughters were devastated, and I was emotionally unavailable to help them through their grief, as I was exhausted and tired from working overtime to pay the bills and care for the girls.

My daughters had to be self-reliant, and I know Melody struggled with this much more deeply than her sisters. She needed more of me than I could give. She became an anxious teenager and rarely stepped out of her comfort zone to try new activities or projects. She was moody and yelled at lot . . ."No!" she screamed a lot, and her sisters avoided her at all costs. Melody was diagnosed with clinical depression and anxiety at age sixteen. Her family doctor said she was sad about losing her dad and was afraid that I might die too. She became very vigilant and hovered at my bedside whenever I was sick. Every time I rolled over in bed, there was her anxious, worried face looking at me.

"Do you want some water, Mom? . . . You have to eat the sandwich I made, or you won't get well . . . Do you need some pills, Mom? . . . Mom, I think you should go to the doctor."

I quickly recognized that I could not show any signs of illness, tiredness, or weakness, as Melody became anxious, moody, and screamed at everyone in the house. I learned to plaster a smile on my face to show that I was well. Again, the lyrics in the ABBA song flooded my mind and were eerily poignant.

Slipping through My Fingers

What happened to the wonderful adventures
The places I had planned for us to go
Well, some of that we did but most we didn't
And why I just don't know.

While sitting at my desk reminiscing about Melody's childhood, I felt God nudging me. *You have to deal with this, Cathy, now! She is sick and needs you.*

I pleaded with God, *I can't. I don't know what to do. I don't want to deal with this right now. I don't know what to say. I don't want to tell anyone.*

I didn't want to tell our family doctor, as she was like a friend to me. She thought I had done amazingly well since my husband passed away, so how could I tell her? She would think badly of me and wonder how I let this happen. She would silently judge me.

I didn't want to tell my family, as they had always told me to slow down. They had encouraged me to spend more time with the girls and would throw my busy lifestyle in my face.

4

I didn't want to tell my church, as they would judge me and gossip about me all *in the name of prayer*. They would say, "If you had prayed enough, this would not have happened to your daughter."

I didn't want to tell my nursing colleagues, as I would be one of those parents we had silently judged. I would be that controlling mother who caused her daughter to rebel against the control and starve herself . . . and I just couldn't take that pain!

*   *   *

I remember walking slowly out to the kitchen and waiting for Melody to come back upstairs. I was sweating. My heart was pounding so hard that my chest hurt. I was shaking uncontrollably. I felt sick to my stomach. I panicked when I heard her come up the stairs. Melody walked into the kitchen; and I murmured a silent prayer, asking for the strength, courage, and wisdom to confront her. I wanted to run away. I wanted to leave it for another time, when I had more courage. I knew that once the words were said, there was no turning back! *I do not feel strong enough for this. Why do I have to do this alone? Why do we have to go through this at all, God? Why us? We had been through enough.*

I tried to swallow past the lump in my throat . . . I took a deep breath and quickly blurted out, "Melody, we need to talk. I don't want you to deny it because I know it's true. You have been throwing up and have lost a lot of weight." *There, I said it. No turning back.* I took another deep breath and swallowed and said, "I want to help you."

Melody stared at me for a moment and then burst into tears. "I have been trying to stop, but I can't. I'm scared, Mom."

I was stunned! I was expecting yelling, stomping out of the room, denial—not a vulnerable, scared, and crying child. Now what was I supposed I do? Instead of my mother's instinct kicking in, my nursing experience took over, and Melody and I talked about the importance of eating and getting vitamins into her body. I was comfortable in my nursing role, and I needed comfort at that moment.

Melody agreed to go to the doctor for a full checkup and have her weight recorded. She also agreed to sit at the table with me for all meals and wait thirty minutes before going downstairs or into a bathroom. We hugged and spent the afternoon shopping for foods she liked and supplements she needed. I believed I could handle this alone. I decided not to tell anyone except our family doctor and hoped all this would be behind us before all the relatives arrived for Melody's high school graduation in the following two months. I believed everything would be okay.

Melody continued to lose weight despite my vigilance and control and was referred to a psychologist. Extended family members arrived for her high school graduation and began discussing Melody's thin body. I brushed it off and said she was just stressed and found myself changing the subject whenever her weight was brought up. When the graduation ceremonies were over and everyone went home, I was relieved, as the stress of lying and making excuses about Melody's weight became unbearable.

Melody's weight dropped significantly after her graduation, and she began displaying bizarre behaviors like opening up cans of food and hiding them in cupboards. I discovered this when we developed a problem with ants. I screamed whenever I opened a cupboard, as ants were swarming all over the open food. The smell in the kitchen was sickening, as there was rotten and decaying food hidden behind dishes and cans. My other daughters were disgusted and started eating meals at their friends' homes. I spent hours crying while hunting for rotten food, cleaning the cupboards, and spraying the bugs. Melody wouldn't talk about it. She said it was part of her eating disorder, and I had to *deal with it.* I remember thinking, *Is it possible to hate your own child?* I struggled with this thought daily as she became more belligerent in our conversations and continued to lose weight.

By September 2005, Melody refused to go to the doctor or psychologist anymore; and I was powerless to do anything, as she was eighteen years old and able to make her own decisions. I was living with a seething anger and an overwhelming fear that we were losing the battle. Our home was a war zone, and no one wanted to be there, myself included. I began working more and more hours per week. I just couldn't face the horror at home. I sensed I was throwing in the towel; and I couldn't even pray for help, as I was worn out physically, emotionally, and spiritually. I stopped crying. I stopped visiting friends, and I sank into a deep depression.

On a cold November day, Melody walked past me, and I gasped! She was a human skeleton! I clamped my hand over my mouth to keep from screaming out loud from the shock. She looked like death . . . I silently screamed, *God, please help her!* I ran into my room, fell on my knees beside my bed, and cried like I have never cried before . . . weeping, wailing, sobbing, which seemed to last for hours. With my heart breaking, I thought, *My daughter is going to die, and I can't go on without her.* I began to pray and bargain the day away. *God, let me die instead or let her live, and I'll help others suffering with this disease. Whatever you want me to do, I will do it. Just please, God, don't take her from me.*

It was at this time I finally realized I had to start being open and honest about her disease and look for the support we needed. I knew that if I didn't, she would die! I took a deep breath, silently prayed for courage, and phoned my pastor. I was amazed at receiving compassion and encouragement instead of judgment. I admitted to him that I was very scared and depressed. This was tough for me to admit, as I was an intensely private person. It was then that my pastor shared with me that his child had suffered an eating disorder as well but was now completely recovered and doing well in life. I couldn't believe it! That meant there was hope for Melody too!

Using my newfound courage, I phoned a close friend and asked if we could go for a walk. I shared with her about Melody's eating disorder, and she hugged me and said, "You have been a great mom. This is not your fault." Relief rushed over me. She didn't condemn me or blame me or admonish me for working too much. I began to realize how important support was! My family and friends became my lifeline, and they built me up whenever I got scared or worried. I was able to be around Melody and find joy in little things.

I convinced Melody to go back to the doctor and was alarmed to discover that her weight had plummeted to a dangerous level.

Her blood pressure was perilously low, and her heartbeat was irregular and very slow. The doctor said she needed to be admitted to the hospital. Melody had not eaten anything in three days and had had no water for twenty-four hours. She was crying but refused to go to the hospital because she didn't want to be force-fed or take medication. I was powerless to make the decision, so I took Melody home.

We lay down on my bed, and I held her in my arms. She was so weak and pale. I was afraid to close my eyes and sleep in case she would die before I woke up. I just lay there and stared at her. Tears were spilling down my face. I offered her a sip of water—no, I *begged* her to take a sip of water.

"I can't, Mom, I can't."
"Please, Melody, just a little. Please . . . for me."
"It hurts, Mom, I can't."

My heart was breaking, and I was trying desperately to hold on to my faith. While Melody slept, I called my pastor, and he sent an urgent prayer request throughout the church. I cried and cried and prayed and began bargaining again with God.

Please, God, let her live . . . I will do whatever you want me to do . . . I'm begging, please, God!

The next morning, while I was pacing in the living room and praying, Melody walked out of the bedroom and started crying. "Mom, I need help. Help me." I was shocked, elated, hopeful, scared. Again, I found solace in the lyrics from ABBA.

Slipping through My Fingers

The feeling that I'm losing her forever
And without really entering her world
I'm glad whenever I can share her laughter
That funny little girl.

*   *   *

I was jolted back to the present when I heard cheering from the bridal party. I realized that Melody had on another beautiful wedding gown. This one was mermaid-style, and she looked stunning. Melody began to cry with joy and declared that this was her gown. She said it had everything she was looking for and was proud of how it showed off her curves. Hearing those wonderful words was a healing balm to my soul . . . Melody is proud of her curves! With hugs and kisses to everyone within hugging and kissing range, we left the bridal shop. Melody suggested a lunch date to celebrate, and we all agreed. I sat and enjoyed watching her eat and once again thought back to a time when this was not possible.

*   *   *

Melody insisted that she didn't want to go to the hospital but to a treatment center instead. She wanted to go where they did not force-feed or drug with pills. She wanted to go where they provided therapy to help her understand why she was doing this. Her nutrition counselor had previously mentioned a treatment center out of province that provided several hours of therapy per day and had an excellent recovery rate for both anorexia and bulimia.

I phoned immediately, and miraculously, they had a bed available. They said they usually have a waiting list, but because it was close to Christmas, one girl had backed out until January. They agreed to take Melody. She was both excited and scared to go, but she said she would stay until she was well. I could not go with Melody to the treatment center, as I had work obligations with no replacement on short notice . . . maybe subconsciously, I was too afraid to go and see other anorexic girls . . . too real . . . too close to home.

I drove Melody to the airport on a cold, snowy morning at the end of November. Melody was frail looking and very pale. She was so skinny that people stared at her when we checked in, and I wanted to yell, "Stop staring and mind your own business!" As soon as Melody received her boarding pass, I told her I had to leave—it was too painful to prolong the good-bye. I hugged her and then left. Just before I went out the door, I turned and looked at her. A deep sadness and fear overwhelmed me. *Is this possibly the last time I would see her? Is she going to die?* Suddenly, I didn't want to leave. *Why am I sending my frail, sick daughter alone to get help? Oh God, I should be going with her! Why didn't I take a leave from work?*

All at once, I hated myself.
I hated my job.
I hated leaving Melody.
I hated everyone and everything at that moment.
But I especially hated myself.

I pushed these thoughts from my mind and smiled bravely at Melody, whispered that I loved her, and turned to walk out of the airport. Before I reached my car, the tears started . . . I cried so hard I couldn't see well enough to drive. I just sat in the car, and tears poured like water down my face and onto my winter coat. I couldn't pray . . . I was too grief-stricken. *What a terrible mother you are*, ran through my head over and over.

Unexpectedly, I heard God's voice in my ear, and I immediately stopped crying. I felt a peace that I had never felt before, and I sensed God telling me Melody would recover, and I just needed to have faith. I dried my tear-stained face, took a deep breath, prayed for Melody, and drove to work. By the time I reached the hospital to work, I was peaceful. I looked forward to phoning Melody when I got home that evening. It was hard to concentrate at work, as I wondered how her flight was and if she managed her connections in her frail state. I had to keep reminding myself of God's word to me in the car. *Melody would recover . . . Melody would recover.* I phoned the treatment center and discovered that Melody had arrived safely and had eaten some dinner. That was the best news I could have received, as she had been refusing food for days at home. God was faithful and answering my prayer!

With encouragement and support from friends and my doctor, I began to cope and live again. As life stabilized, my other daughters spent more time at home, and we began our healing process. Melody also responded well to the therapy and support at the treatment center. We talked frequently on the telephone, and I was encouraged by her commitment to get well. She arrived home in January 2006 with a healthy weight gain and a much better outlook on life. Hallelujah! Melody agreed to see her family doctor and nutrition counselor regularly after arriving home, and with inspiring determination and only a few minor setbacks, she recovered well.

On September 25, 2010, Melody married the love of her life. She was glowing and looked beautiful in her wedding gown. Family and friends came to show their love and support during this blissful time, and with many cheers and tears, our family healing was complete.

Melody and her sisters are very close now. They look forward to holidays to get together, and they talk frequently on the phone. Although this was a difficult time, the process taught me the danger of isolation. I discovered the importance of support—from family, friends, and professionals. The healing process began when I opened up and looked for help for both Melody and our family. I am forever grateful to my extended family for their love and to my friends for their unconditional support and encouragement during this time.

Our journey began when Melody was seventeen years old, and she is now a healthy twenty-four-year-old. I am so proud of the work she has done to get well. She is happy within herself and who she has become as an individual, as well as someone who is married. Her husband is incredibly supportive and loves her as she deserves to be loved.

*I pray that God, the source of hope, will fill you
completely with joy and peace because you trust in him.
Then you will overflow with confident hope through the
power of the Holy Spirit.*

—Romans 15:13

Chapter Two

Shooting Star
Patrice Skovgaard

When Robyn was young, I used to wonder how I got so lucky. She was the perfect child—even-tempered, agreeable, never a discipline problem. She excelled at school in every subject and was popular with classmates and a friend to all. A natural leader and peacemaker, she made the troubles of the world her own and truly cared about what happened to other people in her own little world and globally. She was a gifted athlete and played every sport with grace and speed. Her future seemed assured, and she talked about scholarships to become a doctor or an engineer. Nothing was out of her reach.

Her father and I had divorced when Robyn was four and her sister, Lindsay, was six. After a couple of years, I moved to another city for a better job and a fresh start. As time went on, their father contacted them less and less; and visits became more and more infrequent, partly because of the kids' weekend activities and partly because of their father's inability to maintain a close relationship with them. He had remarried, and the situation there was less than welcoming for the girls.

I was fine with this on the surface. I had also remarried, and the girls were busy and seemed happy. I did not feel that it was my job to maintain their father's relationship with the girls. If he could not be bothered to initiate contact, I did not think I needed to force the issue. I made him aware of upcoming school plays and important sporting events; if he chose not to come, that was his loss.

When I was being honest with myself, I was angry with their father for deserting them. It had been a difficult divorce, and we could no longer speak civilly. I was just as glad not to have to deal with him, while at the same time I agonized that he made less and less of an effort to be a dad. Robyn had felt especially close to him, and while she rarely spoke about it, his absence hurt her.

Robyn and I had always been open with each other. She talked to me about everything. We had good discussions about drugs, smoking, sex, and birth control. We talked about her dad and what she was feeling about him. She had a mature view of things, knew what was right and what was wrong, and seemed to be understanding toward her father. I supported her in everything—going with her to all her games, tournaments, concerts and cheering her on. I was proud of her achievements and of her levelheadedness. I was certain she was on the right path.

When Robyn entered grade nine at high school, things changed. Suddenly, she was a smaller fish in a bigger pond; there were kids who were taller than she was, better and more competitive at sports, and equally as bright. It was hard for her to adapt to this, and while her marks remained high and she still played on as many teams as she could manage, her confidence in herself seemed to slowly fade. She started going out less and letting the phone ring without answering it. The summer after grade nine, she lost her way. She spent a lot of time on her own, bored and restless, rollerblading by herself for hours every day.

That previous spring, she had badly sprained an ankle playing soccer and was out of sports for several weeks. The inactivity combined with ordinary adolescence had caused a minor weight gain. Comments about her weight from unthinking people stung her deeply, and during the summer, she lost all that weight and more. She also decided that she wanted to become a vegetarian. I wasn't totally against this. I brought her home books from the library and worked with her to make sure she would get enough protein and variety in her diet. By the end of the summer, she was slim and fit and ready for grade ten. I told her that she should not lose any more weight. I was so unsuspecting. I was so blind.

There were many things going on in Robyn's mind that she was no longer sharing with anyone. She had written a journal in grade nine as a school assignment, before any of the physical signs of her illness. It was handed in to a teacher for marking on a regular basis. In this journal, she bared her soul. The first line in it was how her father had not called her in several months. Her anguish was clear and spelled out, page after page of pain and sadness. She talked about not eating, about how lost she was feeling, about how she was not good enough, about how much she missed her dad. This journal had been marked by the teacher on several pages. It was a clear cry for help that no one heard. I did not come into possession of this journal until much later after it was written and Robyn was already lost to her illness. Despite my complaints and meeting with the school board, nothing was done other than an assurance that the teacher would now actually read some of the entries instead of just marking them for the amount of content.

*   *   *

As grade ten started, the weight loss did not stop. She became way too thin; she had trouble playing soccer, and it looked like she was running through water. It happened so fast. She went to an out-of-town soccer tournament over Thanksgiving weekend. We had family coming for the weekend, so I did not go with her. Partway through the tournament, I got a phone call. She could not play; she was too sick. One of the moms had caught her throwing up in a bathroom stall. They were sending her home early. I cried that whole night—inconsolable, fearful. The next day, I went and picked her up at the airport, and she spent the rest of the weekend at home. She would not discuss what had happened. She helped to cook Thanksgiving dinner. She sat at the table and picked at her food. I was elated when she had a piece of pumpkin pie. We went to our family doctor, and he confirmed that she was anorexic and gave her a stern talking-to. Robyn sat on his examination table and listened vacantly and smiled as if she thought he was crazy. He referred us to a pediatrician who specialized in eating disorders. We began to see her regularly.

All that fall season, I watched her as best I could. I went to work at 5:30 a.m. and worked until about noon so I could be home for her lunch and dinner. My husband worked evenings and was there to supervise the morning meals. I got home as he was leaving for work. Robyn and I shopped together and tried to find high-calorie foods that she would eat. She carried on all the ritualistic eating disorder behaviors. She would hide food even though I was sitting in front of her, watching her eat. She would hide it in her pockets, on the floor, under her dishes; or she would try to throw it away. Her mealtimes took hours to complete and were torture for all of us.

For a time in the beginning, I thought that I could heal her just with the power of my will. I had always been able to handle everything. I had raised two kids on my own for seven years. I had gone to night school, made a career, bought a house for us, found a loving husband. I had done more than survived—I had flourished. Certainly, I could fix this. Robyn was part of me, and I could fix her. Instead, Robyn turned into a person that I did not even know. Gone was the easy smile, the sparkle in her eyes, the joy in just being able to run fast and kick a ball. She was isolated and secretive; her eyes held nothing but hopelessness. Her bones showed through her paper-white skin. She would seem to be listening to my endless reasoning and encouragement, but it would never break through to her soul. She lied continually, got caught for shoplifting laxatives, missed school, and abused alcohol and drugs. Her life disintegrated.

When I finally came to realize that I had no control over this illness, I lost my mind. I became depressed, anxious, and agoraphobic. I could only leave the house long enough to drive the girls to school and then come home again. And I did that only because Robyn was under doctor's orders not to do any activity and was too weak to walk that distance. I missed six months of work and required weeks of day hospital care and therapy before I recovered enough to get parts of my life back. During that time, I had to learn some difficult lessons. The hardest of these lessons was to believe in my heart that because this illness was not my fault, there would be nothing that I could do to fix it. At best, I could try to keep her safe and keep myself sane.

Robyn continued to starve herself. She was hospitalized a couple of times for several weeks of re-feeding. Her doctor could not give us any good news. When I would plead with the doctor to tell me what to do, her only answer was, "Keep on loving her." Robyn saw a therapist weekly, and she went through several in a couple of years. None of them had any effect. She was completely lost in her obsession. By this time, she was so sick that she could not even imagine another way of living.

I remember snapshots of that time, coming down into the kitchen from a sleepless night to make hot chocolate and finding her there like a little squirrel, making peanut butter toast and eating it by the loaf—unable to stop even when there were others in the kitchen . . . her eyes were glazed and crazed looking as she would lick the peanut butter off the knife in gobs. I remember walking into her bedroom in the morning to wake her for school, finding garbage cans lined with plastic bags and full to the top with vomit and Robyn lying on her bed, too weak to get up. I remember her standing up and fainting onto the hardwood floor, waking up crying and scared. I held her and rocked her there on the floor; she was small like a child, and her bones poked out everywhere. I remember when she was in the school fashion show, modeling swimsuits; and I stayed away, mortified that they would allow her to go out on a stage like that and show off what she considered to be an acceptable body. Her doctor had said it would be okay, but it nearly drove me to panic. I remember sitting in the hospital emergency room with her every Saturday, when she had to go for blood tests, and waiting the hour until the results came back to make sure she didn't have to be admitted. I remember the smell of her body as it slowly consumed itself from the inside out, breaking down muscle and organ tissues for nourishment.

During these years, to try to maintain some sense of reality, my husband and I saw a parent counselor and also attended structured group sessions with other parents of children with eating disorders. It was a release to be able to talk about what was going on with people who understood. The fathers appeared to have an especially hard time with it, and they would voice their frustrations at the meetings. They would describe the things their daughters would do with complete disbelief. We could all relate; the support there was unquestioning. We even sometimes found the power to laugh. Our unofficial mantra became, "Kick 'em in the ass and make 'em eat a sandwich." It was our way of dealing with something that was so far beyond any of our understanding. When things got really serious and there were tears or awkward silences while we all pondered how our children's lives had gone awry, someone would just have to make a reference to our mantra, and the mood in the room would shift immediately. We learned a valuable lesson during those sessions . . . if you can laugh at something and make fun of it, it loses its power to hurt you. I have used that realization at other bleak times in my life, and it has never failed me.

The parent counselor that my husband and I saw as a couple was a warm and wonderful person. A mother of a difficult child herself, she was empathetic and provided us with concepts to think about and tasks to complete between visits. She helped us to try to view the eating disorder as an illness and treat it like any other illness rather than as a behavior issue. And she let us talk; she let us cry, but she would never let us give up. We sat in her office for an hour every week. My husband and I held hands and listened and talked. It was our refuge in a world that our friends and relatives did not understand and no longer wanted to hear about after so much time had passed. My husband was my rock throughout. He is a quiet man and not given to showing a lot of emotion. While he did not understand Robyn's illness, he never backed away from any us. There are two things that can happen to a relationship when a crisis happens: you will either be driven apart into your own sad places, or you will be welded together into one—stronger than you could ever be separately. This is what happened to us. Even through the time I lost myself, he was always there loving me, raising me up, believing in me and in our ability to come through the other side. He saved my life, plain and simple.

*   *   *

Robyn spent three months in a hospital at one point, on bed rest. She had her seventeenth birthday there. I visited her every day, and we would play Chinese checkers and Pop-O-Matic Trouble. I would give her back rubs, and we would talk and cuddle for hours. Sometimes I felt that she was getting better. There were glimpses of my Robyn in there somewhere. There were three, sometimes four, kids with eating disorders in the ward during that time. They would sit at their own little table to eat their meals, and someone would watch them eat and supervise them for half an hour after that to make sure they kept it down. The nursing staff would sometimes talk about them, and as Robyn's room was right by the nursing station, she would hear everything they said. Once, one of the nurses made a comment that she wished they would leave so they could have more room for the kids that were really sick. While I was quite angry when I heard about this, I realized over time that this was typical of the attitude of many health care professionals, especially those who were not directly involved with the kids with eating disorders. A lot of them seemed to think that it was just an attempt to get attention, that the girls were just being stubborn. They believed there was really nothing wrong with them, and they had the ability and control to end their illness whenever they wanted.

When Robyn left the hospital, she was at an acceptable weight, and I loved to look at her. I could hardly take my eyes off her. I felt she was safe for the first time in years. It did not last, as she began to lose weight again almost immediately. On her eighteenth birthday, she moved out into her own apartment so she could starve in peace. She had quit school and managed to find a job and support herself.

I was terrified. I made a rule that she had to phone me every day. By some miracle, she agreed to this, and we kept in touch this way.

It was actually somewhat of a relief for the rest of the family not to have her living at home; we did not have to watch the destruction firsthand. But the worry never ended. A few times when I could not get a hold of her, I would be out of my mind until I found her or she called me. One time, I had her landlady unlock her apartment door for me because she wasn't answering her phone for hours and wasn't at work. I was sure that I would find her dead. When she was there, alive, I collapsed onto the floor in her hallway and sobbed, too distraught to even care who saw or heard me.

Robyn was so tiny during those first few months away from home. She was at her lowest weight ever. I do not know how she even functioned. As she was eighteen, there was not a lot I could do. At one point, she was so ill that her doctor and I had her committed to the psychiatric unit of the hospital. Her potassium levels were dangerously low, which could lead to heart failure. During her seventy-two-hour mandatory stay, she was given supplementary potassium to boost her levels. She would not eat the hospital food, sick as she was; so I scrounged things she would eat from the hospital cafeteria, mostly just vegetables. She was admitted on the Friday of a long weekend, and no doctors visited her until the following Monday. She phoned me in the middle of the night during that weekend to say that she didn't feel right; her arms and legs were numb. There was no way to get a hold of anyone in the ward overnight, so I told her to just hang in there until morning. When she finally did see a doctor, it was found that she had been overdosed on potassium, a potentially fatal mistake. When her seventy-two hours' forced confinement was over, I was just as happy to see her out of there as she was to get out. We did not try that again.

*   *   *

I went to the funeral for a young woman from our neighborhood. We had known her through the eating disorders association in our city, and her siblings went to my daughters' school. She had been sick for years, unreachable, and her body finally just gave out. As her mother walked down the church aisle at the end of the service, cradling the urn holding her daughter's ashes, I saw myself in her face. Two more girls from our city died that same year from eating disorders.

I felt like I was living a double life. On one side, I was holding it all together, going to work, spending time with my family. I would pretend that it didn't bother me that Robyn was never there for Easter dinner or Christmas dinner or any other family occasion where food was involved. I would get up every day, get dressed, and head off to do whatever needed to be done. On the other side, I was falling apart, trying to accept the fact that Robyn was going to die. On this side of life, there was no hope. I would cry uncontrollably, huge animal sobs from down in my gut. I slept poorly and would stare into space for hours. I had written her obituary in my mind and had picked out the music that would be played, songs about angels and being free. I was preparing for the inevitable. I had no control over which side of life I would wake up in on any given day.

Robyn only had one side to her life—her eating disorder. For years, she was no more than a wraith, transparent and so insubstantial I was afraid to look away from her, fearing I would not be able to see her when I looked back. She was living; but she was floating, anchorless, going through the motions in her own shadow land. Her illness controlled her life completely—from where she worked, to who her friends were, to how she spent her free time. Sometimes there were glimpses of hope. She went to night school for a couple of semesters and completed some of her courses toward her high school diploma. She got a cat, and she had a boyfriend. She started making beautiful jewelry and signed up for a goldsmith's course, which would count toward her diploma. But that only lasted a few months, and she did not finish. Once again, she disappeared back to her own world.

As Robyn approached her mid twenties, she became somewhat more open about her illness. She gained some weight—not because she was getting better, but because she had switched from anorexia and bulimia to full-time bulimia. She would no longer cover the self-inflicted cuts to her legs and arms, another obsession she had cultivated in her early years. I was reaching the end of my tolerance. I had watched her suffer and make so many bad decisions for so many years. I was tired of living in fear that she would die. I started to talk to her about treatment programs. She went back to therapy and made some progress with a therapist that she connected with. It was painfully slow, but things were changing. In the meantime, she struggled with alcoholism, drugs, and bad relationships that demeaned her and slowed her realization that she had value and control over her own life and her own destiny.

When Robyn became more open about her illness, she began revealing to me in small bits the things that had been invading her mind from an early age. From the time she was about ten years old, she had a poor body image of herself. She started cutting herself when she was eleven. She was so nervous about failing at the beginning of races that she would sometimes hyperventilate and be unable to finish. She started going to secret drinking parties during junior high. Her first boyfriend was a drug dealer. I thought I knew my child. I thought that she told me everything, but I did not know her at all.

I had not seen Robyn eat in years. It was just something that she did in private. When she told me that she had started eating at work in front of people, I was amazed. This was true progress! I knew there was real hope when she and her boyfriend stopped in one day and brought food with them, as they had been out all afternoon and hadn't stopped to eat. Robyn plunked herself down on the rug and ate a veggie wrap right there, with no self-consciousness or hesitation. I just sat there and made small talk, afraid that I would say something or look at her wrong, and she would stop eating. When she left, I ran around the house cheering! I started inviting her for family dinners, and sometimes she would come. Her sister and I kept talking to her about going for treatment. She would agree that this was something she had to do but then found any number of excuses why she could not go right now. It was always something that she viewed as being in the future. These talks usually ended with her getting angry and running away. While there were indications that she was improving, we all knew this was not something that she could do for herself. Finally, when she was twenty-four, she agreed to go for treatment. She took leave from her work and went to a live-in treatment center in August 2008. She was there for four months and made great progress. When she came home in December, she was a different person. Even her voice was different, more confident and more mature.

Robyn is now twenty-five. She is over a year self-injury free and is no longer a practicing bulimic. She has begun to take care of herself physically and willingly sees a doctor and a dentist. She got her driver's license and will soon have her high school diploma. After that, university will follow. She is building solid friendships and is learning to control other self-destructive behaviors. There will always be an eating disorder, but her own self-awareness and maturity will keep her from going back. Once again, at long last, there are no limits to her present or her future. She is free.

I have spent many, many hours analyzing what happened to my perfect child that took away so many years of our lives and wasted them to this illness. I still feel guilty—not because I think I caused it, but because I have missed so much of my own life and the life of my older daughter, Lindsay. I will always have these regrets. Lindsay has also suffered. She has been angry and hurt, but in her own adulthood, she now understands and can reason it out. The true cause of Robyn's eating disorder comes from herself. She felt abandoned by her father and, as part of her therapy, has spoken with him and resolved this issue between them. They are now quite close and speak to or text each other often. Other causes are simply genetic; Robyn was born to feel too much. As Lindsay said to me just recently, it's like she has no skin. She feels too deeply, cares too much. She never learned to be resilient, to let things bounce off. No one has control over this.

Similarly, no one has true control over recovery. There were years and years of Robyn's life when she was unable to think clearly, unable to heal. She knew when the time was right to come back. No matter how much I cared, how many tears I shed, how much money was spent on treatment, the only thing that would cure her illness was her own readiness to be cured. Robyn was a star, a brilliant shooting star. Her illness snuffed out that light completely. But now, years later, her light shines again—not as brightly as before, but steady and enduring.

Give all your worries and cares to God, for he cares about you.

—1 Peter 5:7

Chapter Three

Our Million-Dollar Family
Tina Kulifaj

The year was 1990. February was almost over, and I was awaiting the birth of our second child. She finally arrived just a few days after my due date. Life could not have been better. My husband, Dale, and I were blessed with a baby boy and then, three years later, our beautiful baby girl. Many referred to us as the "million-dollar family." We both had good jobs, a great relationship, a nice home, and an abundance of good friends and family nearby. What more could anyone ask for? With all that going for us, raising children should have been a piece of cake . . . or so we thought. I knew we'd experience some bumps along the way, but I was completely confident that we'd handle them with little or no difficulties. If I only knew that the most challenging job of my life was about to begin! We soon learned that when it came to parenting, what worked for our son, Scott, would most often not work for Carly. They were two completely different individuals. He was happy-go-lucky and outgoing, and she was much more shy and sensitive. I joked that Carly was my Velcro kid because she stuck so close to me.

As an infant, Carly had colic. This was the first test of our parenting skills and our relationship as husband and wife. Anyone who has experienced raising a baby with colic would agree that instead of savoring the time with your infant, you somehow wish that you could magically fast-forward it to the point where your baby outgrows the colic. It was very hard for me to watch Carly cry endlessly. Most babies are content directly after being fed, but not Carly—it was the opposite. This was her most miserable time. She finally recovered from colic at about eight months. Perfect! We made it through the bump in the road. Life handed us a challenge, and we emerged victorious.

Time marched on, and our family life was peaceful. Both kids were doing well in school, taking part in their chosen activities, and each had a nice circle of friends. Our next bump was just around the corner . . . middle school. There was a period of time when Scott, our once happy-go-lucky young man, took on a new middle school-influenced persona complete with a bad attitude. Somehow we nipped it in the bud, and our once respectful kid returned. Dale and I felt that we had a grasp on what middle school was all about and were ready to handle the challenges Carly would face there too. When she entered grade seven, she was terrified as she often was of anything unknown. Carly was out of her comfort zone in a place where shyness and social anxiety are qualities that make a tough situation even tougher. We began to notice a dramatic change in her personality midway through grade seven. Our conversation around the dinner table was very brief when it was Carly's turn to answer questions. We were accustomed to some sort of response about what she was learning in science that day or who she hung out with at lunch, but suddenly, her answer to each of these questions was only a shoulder shrug—no eye contact . . . no smile. We also noticed Carly's makeup changing to a very dark and, in my opinion, scary look. Hoodies became the staple of her wardrobe. The hood was always pulled up over her head so that her face couldn't be seen. Most of her clothes were black. *Where did my daughter go?* I wanted her back!

I felt as if I didn't even know this person at our table. As soon as dinner was over, she would leave and head straight upstairs to her room. She turned her music up very loud . . . . horrible lyrics . . . horrible messages . . . how could anyone listen to that stuff? If you weren't depressed before listening to it, you were bound to be after!

In the days to come, there was a lot of crying. I would hear it start shortly after Carly went upstairs to her room. I would knock on the door; sometimes she let me in, and other times, she did not. When she did let me in, I found her rolled up in a ball, tissue upon tissue beside her and eyes puffy and red, with mascara everywhere. When I asked what was wrong, the response was often a shoulder shrug . . . There was never a defined answer like, "I had a fight with my friend" or "I failed a test today." Eventually, she started saying that she hated herself. This, I was not prepared for. I had always encouraged my kids to be proud of who they were, treat others with respect, and just do their best at whatever it was they were doing—and everything else would fall into place.

Things weren't falling into place at all; in fact, they were falling apart. At times, my husband and I became very angry with each other. This was very uncommon for us, but we were emotionally depleted from our jobs and came home knowing the stress level was going to rise dramatically once we got there. Our once happy home seemed like a prison to everyone living in it. There were times that we both felt like leaving to escape from the madness and sadness . . . but we knew we simply could not. We were the parents, and our kids desperately needed us. *Where did we go wrong?* was a question we often asked ourselves. *What is happening to our million-dollar family?*

This pain went on for weeks, yet I had not seen any behavior that indicated we were dealing with an eating disorder until one fateful day when Carly called me in to her room and told me that she had just vomited but didn't know why. I asked her if she felt sick or "fluish," but her answer was no. Believe it or not, I still didn't clue in that this was the beginning of her eating disorder. I mean, why would she tell me that she vomited if she made herself do it? It just didn't make sense to me. Surely, she wouldn't want me to know that. I naively believed that this was an isolated incident. I couldn't have been more wrong. It was soon after that I realized we had a real problem on our hands. Every night became the same ritual: little or no conversation, up to the washroom after dinner, music playing loudly, back into the room, and endless hours of crying.

My daughter had full-blown bulimia. She was living this hell; and I, her mother, couldn't fix it. All I was able to do was hand her more tissue when she cried, rub her back, and tell her over and over again that she was beautiful. I didn't know what else to do. I felt so helpless.

* * *

Walking was a stress reliever for me, and fortunately, it was the one thing that Carly agreed to do with me. Many an evening, I made her get her jacket on and go out for a thirty-minute walk with me. Sometimes we had a conversation and other times not. I knew she needed more help than I could offer, but I didn't know where to start. I was quite certain she wouldn't want to leave home and to go to a treatment center; and because of her shy, highly sensitive nature, I was not even sure if she would agree to help from a professional. I didn't want to push her into anything, yet I knew it had to be done. I think she enjoyed our walks because she was able to talk openly without eye contact, as that was hard for her. The same held true for our times together in the car. She shared information more freely on these rides, and I was relieved and happy to tap into something that worked for us both. We were able to have some deep conversations. To my surprise, during one of our walks, Carly broached the subject of her eating disorder and begged me to get her help. She wanted it all to stop but couldn't do it on her own.

As parents, it was our responsibility to seek help . . . our daughter was relying on us. Dale and I spoke to our colleagues at work and were humbled by their reactions. I was expecting to get the big surprised-sounding "Oh my gosh," but instead, my coworkers were completely empathetic to our situation and not as shocked as I expected them to be. Dale encountered the same reaction from his coworkers. One of his coworkers revealed that his daughter had gone through the same thing as Carly, and he offered words of encouragement and passed on the name of a counselor that he claimed saved his daughter's life. My boss encouraged me to take whatever time off I needed to be with Carly, and one of my

to eat, and that was that . . . I spent the night worrying and praying (hard). It was the first of many nights like this. I had told her that she wouldn't solve anything by not eating. Then I begged her to eat! It was with great relief that Ali came to the kitchen the next morning asking for some french toast. I was elated and got the bread out . . . Hallelujah! This absurdity was over. Right . . . who was I kidding? I think that even Ali knew this was not the way to go. She knew that not eating wouldn't solve her problems, but she really didn't know what to do. All she did know was that she wasn't happy. I worried about her all the time. Then I told myself not to worry about her because she had always been so good—such a good girl, great grades in school, nice friends, popular, played her sports well.

I know now that her heart was sad . . . thinking and writing about it is something that is very difficult for me. It took me a while to even begin to understand how little I knew of her suffering. I remember her counselor's words to me: "You don't know how bad it is for Ali. She never sleeps through the night. She is scared and sad."

When your child has an eating disorder, lying becomes the norm. They lie to you, and you lie to yourself. Mealtimes are a euphemism. What is a mealtime? I became obsessed with Ali's eating. What was she eating? How much? If she ate, I told myself things were okay—as if that particular symptom of her illness was a sign of her mental health. If she told me she was fine, I believed her because I wanted her to be fine. But the truth is it is not until the eating disorder is acknowledged and addressed that there will be any peace, healing, or recovery. As her mother, I learned to live with the fear. I learned to accept that I was part of the problem regardless of why it exists because I needed to be part of the care and the solution. I needed to listen to people who could help and let them do their work no matter how much I thought I knew best. The world that my daughter was living in was her reality, whether I knew it existed or not.

One day, my daughter came to me and asked me if I would go to see a movie with her. I was surprised and asked what movie she wanted to see. She said *Stepmom* and then added, "Dad said he will go if you will." I was a little taken aback but agreed to go, and the three of us saw the movie. Later, I asked what it was about this film that she liked so much, and she said that she liked the part where the daughter of the couple divorcing yelled at her parents and told them that no one ever asked her what she wanted. No one ever asked her if she wanted to move or have divorced parents. No one had ever thought about how she would feel. When she described the movie, she said it was about a girl whose parents were divorced, whose dad had a girlfriend that everybody hated, and whose mom had cancer. At the time, I was recovering from breast cancer. Ali told her father and me quite a bit about her feelings by taking us to see that movie.

With feelings of guilt, I mulled over Ali growing up in a broken home . . . a very broken home. Her father and I separated when she was only seven. I now think that she spent her little girlhood longing for a family. When she became so unhappy and depressed that she developed an eating disorder, I blamed myself and her father. Ali had to deal with all the classic problems children of divorced parents go through, which she did valiantly until it just got too hard. Then she crumbled under all the pressure—or at least that is my guess. Ali's father and I did not agree on everything while raising Ali and her brother. When her father and I separated, she was seven, and her brother was nine. The kids spent time with us equally, but it wasn't easy, and they must have felt torn most of the time. Ali and her brother, despite having divorced parents, did not grow up without a father figure. Their dad was a very dominant presence. He had specific ideas about how they would spend their time, what activities they would be involved in, and what standards were expected at school. This caused conflict between him and me. He insisted on the top level of achievement regardless of the activity. I saw the stress on the kids.

The friction was compounded by the different lifestyles that he and I had. Ali's dad was a pilot who would come and go. When he was in town, he had nothing but free time. I was working, going to school, and trying to get back on my feet after the divorce. I never had a day off. I resented him scheduling all of our lives around his.

The kids were aware of this. It was something that they lived with from early on, and most of the time, we were able to make it work. Looking back, I think that the kids lived with the constant pressure of always trying to keep everyone happy.

Ali's high school years were relatively happy. She hung out with a nice group of friends, and I was relieved that I didn't have to worry about her going around with the wrong crowd. She also went on lots of dates and had boyfriends, which convinced me that many of her struggles originated from her broken family life. I felt like a real loser.

One summer, when Ali was seventeen, she got a job scooping ice cream cones. It was a fun job, and her good friend worked there too. She decided that she needed to look skinny for the job and stopped eating again for a while; nevertheless, it wasn't the anorexia that took hold of Ali again . . . she had moved on to bulimia. And it became her enemy. I discovered this when one night, after she had gone out to eat dinner with some friends, she came home and threw up. I heard her in the bathroom and went in to ask if she was okay. She said that she had eaten something that didn't agree with her. I helped her clean up, and she went to bed. I was oblivious . . . I hadn't even thought of bulimia yet.

A few days later, I thought I heard Ali throwing up again. We lived in a town house, and her room and bathroom were on the lower level. I tried to listen by the stairs, but the water was running, and of course, the door was closed—and locked. I decided I was wrong. I must be wrong—she wouldn't throw up on purpose. This went on for a while as I wavered between suspecting the truth and convincing myself that I was wrong. I so desperately wanted to be wrong, but I knew I was right. My daughter was bulimic. I couldn't admit it to myself. I wanted it to go away. I wanted to be wrong.

In addition to the bulimia, Ali had become moody, frequently angry, and verbally abusive. I remember wondering what I had done to make her hate me like this. Her unhappiness ate away at me. She didn't seem to enjoy anything anymore. That summer, my younger brother got married; and Ali traveled to attend the wedding, which was held at my mother's summer home. Ali had been there a few times as a little girl. She always had fun with her cousins, and I was hoping that she would enjoy it. While we were there, she was withdrawn and spent a lot of time sleeping. She just seemed miserable. She later told me that she was scared to go because she knew that she would have to eat, and she didn't know how she was going to be able to purge. She was frantic about this and, of course, had no one to tell. I had no idea that she was agonizing over this. At one point, I tried to talk to her; she said that she hated it there and wished she hadn't come with me, that she didn't care about the wedding and wanted to go home. She hated me for making her go. The whole event was just another thing to *get through* on this rough road. There weren't very many good days when Ali was fighting this disease. You are the support person who is told to be there and to keep praying. And guess what? That is exactly what you do. And it isn't easy. But you have to trust and ask for help.

As a nurse, I had worked a bit in the psychiatric unit, so I hunted through my old psych textbooks looking for information and help. My fear increased when I remembered some of the severely ill young women with eating disorders I had cared for, as I knew that this illness would be harder to deal with if it was given a chance to become firmly entrenched. I was so scared. This was the kind of scared that made me cold all the time, the kind of scared that wouldn't let me think about anything else. I could hardly think about what I was supposed to be doing at work. My stomach was sick, and my mouth was dry. I was too scared to cry, even though I tried to. *Why is my daughter doing this? What is so bad in her life that she has to do this?* These were the questions that had no answers, so I remained scared. One day, while working at the hospital, I cornered our family doctor and said I needed to talk. When I told him about Ali, he asked, "What is she, a ballerina or a gymnast?" I said that Ali was a figure skater. He said, "Oh, that too." But it was more than that. I had all kinds of theories and a vague but tortured picture in my mind of what could be eating away at my daughter. I just couldn't name it, and I didn't know how to help her; and with little optimism from our doctor, I knew it was up to me to seek the support she needed to win this battle.

I made a plan. Ali was going to go to a counselor, and she was going to get well. There would be no negotiation . . . so with carefully chosen words, I entered her room. Her moods had been labile for a while, and I knew this would not be easy. I took a deep breath for courage and said, "I know you have been bingeing and throwing up and need help." Ali denied it. I told her not to bother lying because I knew what she was doing. I told her that she could object all she wanted, but she was going to get help. I was prepared for the battle. I mean, who cares? At this point, I would try anything. All of a sudden, Ali began to cry and admitted that each time I had begged her to tell me what was wrong, it had been this, but she couldn't tell me. Relief rushed over me, with the hope that this confession might bring about the beginning of change. But it was short-lived as her next words were, "Don't bother with me and don't waste any money getting help because I am not worth it!"

I was stunned by Ali's comment and told her that she was a special girl and that I loved her and so did lots of other people. I told her that she could think whatever she wanted of herself, but that I was not going to let her continue to hurt herself, that I would not let her go on like this. After much discussion, she agreed to go for help. I hoped that we had hit bottom, as I was sure that we could not get much lower . . . maybe we had . . . but if we did, we stayed there for a while. I was convinced that there was only person who could help Ali. I felt that way because everyone in our little town who knew anything about this illness had recommended a specific nutrition counselor. We went to see Christina, and she saved Ali.

Christina told me later that every time a new girl comes to see her, she looks at her and says a silent prayer. She asks God to show her how she can help this girl. It took a long time, and it wasn't easy. As trite as it may sound, there are no words for what Christina did for Ali. I truly believe that God put them together. She spent time with all of us—Ali, me, her father—at first and also met and spent time with her brother, who was attending university in Alaska at the time. She described her condition to us as much as possible, always protecting Ali's confidences. We knew that we were in for the long haul. That was okay with me. I told her that Ali's dad would be happy to pay. Ali did her part. She was a good student/client/patient. I think she knew early on that Christina could help her. She learned about the physical attributes of her illness and what she needed to do to deal with it. She kept journals and worked in workbooks. She saw Christina every week. When Ali moved away, she came back to see her frequently, and they also had phone appointments. Ali didn't talk to me about what went on during those visits . . . and to this day, I don't care . . . I just know she's better.

Ali also saw a psychiatrist who diagnosed her with situational clinical depression. Consequently, she took antidepressants for a while; and although she hated them, they probably helped her through some dark times. It is generally thought that a combination of counseling and drug therapy is the best way to treat an eating disorder. The therapy and medication seemed to help, but Ali disliked being treated as a nutcase. Ali saw Christina on a weekly basis until she graduated from high school. She learned a lot about nutrition and how to keep her body healthy, but she continued to struggle all the time. Recovery is slow and painful. When she seemed better, I was hopeful. When she seemed to be regressing, I was panicked. Her progress was always so fragile, which kept me on edge much of the time. I worried that some little thing would set her back. During her last year of high school, there were so many events and parties. I wanted her to get through them all without any disappointments or heartaches. At one point, we went shopping for a grad dress. We found a beautiful dress, and when the time came for the big night, Ali tried on her dress to make sure it looked just right. It seemed a teeny bit tighter than it had been, and I was thinking I might have to take it out a bit. When I said it seemed okay, she became very angry and asked, "How can you say that? Are you saying that I had gained weight?" I held my breath, and the moment seemed to pass.

After Ali graduated from high school, she moved away to attend university. She lived in a dorm her first year and off campus with a friend the second year. She struggled there too. She wasn't well when she left home; she wasn't ready to go. I worried that it was a mistake. I tried to weigh the risk of her living away against the disappointment of having to stay at home when she wanted so desperately to go. So she went. It was probably a mistake. She fought with her bulimia and her depression. She struggled with her schoolwork, and she was lonely. Her time away took its toll. Christina continued to be her lifeline. She came and went from home for the next few years, and school was always hanging over her head. She dreaded her class work and didn't progress well. She wasn't really sure what she wanted to do or what she wanted to be. That was just another stressor for her. The first few years did not go well. After struggling for a while and living with different roommates, not really unlike other college kids, Ali moved in with an old friend from her hometown.

Fortunately, her old friend was a solid and positive influence, and Ali found joy in that. She seemed to be mending. She was twenty years old by then. During all of Ali's struggles with depression and bulimia, her friend remained true and supportive. For me, that was a source of relief because I worried about her when she was away from home. *Is she eating? Is she partying? Is that good or bad? How often should I call? How often should I visit?* I wanted so very badly for her to be happy. There is the notion that these are the happiest, funniest times of one's life. I think that may be skewed more often than we know.

The eating disorder was the ugly manifestation of depression. It was a symptom that became an obsession. My own obsession was trying to figure out why. As the mother, I tried to understand what was hurting her. I tried to understand why she couldn't be happy. What caused the void? What could fill it? What had hurt her so much that she couldn't get past it? As a child, Ali was tough. She had a lot on her plate, and she always accomplished it all. Even then, I worried that she had too many responsibilities. My objections were met with scorn. Then I worried that I hadn't stood up for her enough and allowed her to be pushed too hard. So I blamed myself for that too. In the end, blaming is a worthless activity. It is only love and support that will help. This is what all the books say. I could do that. Over time, Ali figured it out. I had talked with another mom at our church whose daughter had been anorexic for several years. Her daughter was now doing well. When I asked her what had finally helped, she said that her daughter just got tired of being sick. Of course, we both knew that that wasn't all there was to it, but people do get well. They do recover.

Ali is a survivor.

She is tough, but also had support to aid in her recovery; she was blessed with a counselor that knew just how to help her. Her counselor got it. Ali also had her family to support her through the difficult times—each of us in our own way. She knows that she is loved. There is a saying, "The things that don't kill you will make you stronger." Ali is stronger, but she is fragile too. She is human. A few years ago, she ran a marathon in Honolulu, and then she ran one in Vancouver. She did well enough to qualify for the Boston Marathon. Last year, she ran that and finished it on swollen, sore feet.

Yes, she is a survivor.

Now that Ali has her own beautiful little girl, she knows the love that a mother has for her child. It overpowers her; she is a woman of great emotion. Now I think she knows how much I love her. Ali is a great mom. She has chosen to stay home with her baby as long as she can. She is very fortunate to have this option. Her husband agrees that this is what they want to do. Her baby is healthy and happy. I think she will make wise choices for her child (and she hopes for more kids).

Ali was sick for a long time. I think that any illness that goes on for years is a long one. I have been told that an eating disorder is a chronic illness. If the causes were to recur, then the illness may manifest itself again. I think that Ali has dealt with her demons. I am still filled with sorrow remembering her suffering. That cannot change, but I know that she is okay now.

Ali recovered because she had help and was loved. She may have recovered anyway. I am sure some have done it. However, help and love doesn't hurt. Prayers, a counselor (the best), doctors, and family support all played a part in Ali's recovery. I think too that when she realized how much she was loved and supported, she started to love herself again. Getting better will not provide her with a perfect life; however, it will provide her with the tools she needs to help her through life's journey with all that happens in the course of a normal life.

Ali has tremendous faith, as do I. I thank my own mother for that. She and her husband have a Christian home, and God is blessing them, and I know that He will be there always for Ali too.

Faith is the confidence that what we hope for will actually happen; it gives us assurance about things we cannot see.

—Hebrews 11:1

Chapter Five

Just for Today, Do It for You
Dolores Elliott

During the first decade of my daughter's life, Denise was a very sweet, adorable little girl, always wanting to please everyone she came into contact with. She was the youngest of three daughters, and these early years of growth and development were uneventful. My husband and I considered our lives blessed, and we were proud that all three girls had lots of natural talent and athletic ability. Their personalities were unique, with a few common traits, yet Denise was the perfectionist and high achiever. Little did we know she was constantly comparing herself with her sisters and striving to be *just that much better*. Denise succeeded at everything she pursued; we were amazed at her ability to be a successful scholar and athlete. Many doors opened for her!

All this began to change when Denise was about eleven years old. She expressed a deep sadness and told me she was fat. This comment was spoken regularly and troubled me so much so that I took her to the doctor. Just as I suspected, the doctor told her she was not fat as her height and weight were normal on the growth percentile chart. We departed from the doctor's office, and I foolishly thought that would be the end of those comments.

For the next few years, Denise seemed to excel in everything she did. School was a breeze; and before we knew it, she was in grade eight. Denise set her standards very high at everything she pursued; she was involved with soccer, baseball, competitive swimming and dancing, modeling, and the odd job as an extra with a talent agency. Denise was dancing twenty-plus hours a week and tells me now she was always watching herself in the mirror, criticizing different parts of her body and thinking that she was fat. She joined a modeling agency, as her sisters had done a few jobs in the past and enjoyed the new experience. The modeling agency told her she would be a good model to send to Japan, but this was not something her father or I wanted her do. Our reluctance to let her go was validated when it was suggested that Denise *lose just an inch around her hips*. A meal plan was given to follow; it didn't seem harmful, as it practiced healthy eating habits and was not much different from how she was already eating. I really didn't see the next phase coming when Denise began to lose some weight without me realizing what was really going on. She was receiving compliments from her friends at school about how great she looked . . . news I discovered much later.

Denise was very popular with her friends from elementary school and soon had a new set of friends in high school. The high school counselor suggested Denise go into a program for gifted students so that she could accomplish her school day in a shorter period of time and dance for the last half of each day. Although Denise loved to dance, the focus of the program was solely on her dance, and we were sorry that she chose this route because she didn't give any thought of participating in extracurricular activities at school except in soccer. Denise continued to lose weight but loved the girls and playing soccer, as it was part of what made her happy. After taking a hard hit in a game, we made a trip to the emergency department to have her ankle examined. She was diagnosed with a fracture and would be out of soccer. I began to question whether there was a relationship between the condition of her bones, her weight loss, and lack of periods. Knowing what we know now, a more balanced life would have been better, including fewer dance classes and more involvement in school activities.

It is important to mention we had many close family members die in a short period of time, which affected Denise deeply. My father was a big part of Denise's earlier years and passed away when she was just six years old. A few years later, two of my grandparents also passed away. They lived in our community and were very close to Denise. Our much-loved family dog, Nicky, also passed away, leaving an emptiness and sadness in our home. This prompted our family to begin searching for a new dog, and Denise took this task on and very quickly found a litter of puppies. We chose our new family member, and a few weeks later, we brought Tyra home. Of course, I was hoping that this would fill the void and erase the pain that Denise had been so frequently exposed to; but sadly, Denise's last great-grandparent passed away. We were very close to this wonderful lady, and she was the heartbeat in our family. I was so focused on Nanny's last few months that I dismissed what was going on with Denise during this time. While I knew she was struggling, I had no idea how seriously ill she was. I simply didn't have the energy to help her. I wish someone could have realized what was happening to Denise, but there was such a lack of awareness then that any close family members or friends had no idea what was happening to her. Around the same time, a couple of Denise's girlfriends' fathers also suddenly passed away. These losses affected her in a profound way. Denise didn't express her sadness or emotions and seemed to accept death in a very mature manner.

It was after these losses that I noticed Denise's gradual dislike of potatoes with meals, but I accepted this as normal behavior for a girl her age. Her two older sisters had also experienced occasional food dislikes, so why would we question this one with Denise? Denise was becoming obsessed with weighing and measuring herself. Denise later told me she was totally in control of her food and ate only what she allowed herself to eat . . . I was totally oblivious to this. She made her portion sizes smaller and smaller. Next was the exclusion of pasta. This was a clear indication that something was going on, so I took her to the doctor to get some help. Since our family doctor had retired, we saw a new one, who thought that Denise should see a dietician. This appointment was clearly a waste of time, as it consisted of looking at tables of food in empty cartons and the Canadian food guide to see what servings a healthy child and adult needs. We went away extremely discouraged and feeling it was no help at all. Denise was a very bright girl and already knew what her body needed—she didn't need to learn how to weigh and measure her food!

Denise was given a job to model an outfit in a mall store window. Sadly, I drove her to the job, knowing in my heart this was not in her best interest. Denise was quiet in the car; my wish now would be to take this moment back in time and tell her she is not well and can't do the job. Denise met with the store manager, and I didn't see her again until she was in the store window wearing the chosen outfit. My heart sank with heaviness, as she looked too sickly thin. A couple of ladies passed by and made a rude comment about her, and I immediately wanted to take her home to spare the pain. My husband and I decided that this was the last modeling job she would have. It was clear that this agency was not looking out for the best interest of its models. Denise was done with the modeling industry.

After another visit to the doctor, we were told that Denise needed to come in more frequently for monitoring, and an appointment with a psychotherapist was scheduled. Weeks later, amid weigh-ins and more weight loss, Denise went to her first appointment with the recommended psychotherapist. This was how part of the summer vacation was spent. I never would have guessed we would be going from appointment to appointment. Over the next few months, Denise attended all the scheduled appointments, but it was only a matter of time when she divulged that she had no connection with this psychotherapist and did not want to continue the visits. She warned and threatened that Denise needed to see her, or Denise would most likely be in the hospital within a few weeks. Both Denise and I were determined this was not the case, and in desperation, I read somewhere about negative self-talk and how it is a voice that silently takes over every waking minute and increases in its tempo and loudness until this is all the person suffering with an eating disorder (ED) is hearing. All other voices of family, friends, doctors, and others are barely audible. This helped give me a little more understanding of the ED.

That summer came and went with Denise getting more and more sick with ED. Visits to the doctor became more frequent for weigh-ins, blood pressure checks, and lab work. My job as a nurturing mother transformed into a caregiver. Meanwhile, I could not show how worried I was about her state of ill health and looked forward to each new day, always with a stiff upper lip, thinking we are going to beat this horrible illness. I spent many quiet moments sobbing, worrying, and praying that she would somehow find the lost link and connect with someone to give her the hope and courage to fight the eating disorder and help her discontinue the serious restricting and over exercising.

The following month's examination results made us realize that Denise's health was compromised, and therefore, a request to the children's hospital was sent from the new pediatrician on her case. Our experience with this doctor was rather annoying, as every time I took Denise for an appointment, he would speak to me as if she was not in the room or talk to her like she was a four-year-old child. This was so frustrating for both Denise and myself; we would leave even more discouraged after the way he treated her. We were informed there was a waiting list for the hospital program, and Denise should try to maintain her weight! Not sure if that was possible . . . I was doing my best not to be the food police and to watch what she was eating, but she was so clever with being a step ahead of me—for example, wanting to fix the meals with or without me and then claiming to have eaten earlier and that she wasn't hungry. I didn't realize at the time that this was the ED voice that had been telling her that she has had enough to eat and doesn't need or maybe deserve any more. How sad, when I look back, that this illness entrenched this sort of thought process in her head without anyone able to address it.

In the fall of 2000, my daughters Tanis and Denise returned to school, and Leanne worked and planned her extended journey to Australia. Both of Denise's sisters became concerned when their friends mentioned how thin Denise was. I continued to hope things would turn around, but after a couple of months, I realized this was more than we could handle. I was frustrated and worried about Denise's lack of insight about what was going on, but I too was struggling to understand eating disorders or how it happens, as I had never been around anyone with an eating disorder. My doctor didn't know how to help us but believed having a weekly talk and weigh-in was necessary. There were no support groups to attend; it was such a lonely place for Denise, her sisters, and us. Denise's friends didn't know how they could help either. Our home atmosphere was overflowing with tension; simple conversation was guarded, and it felt like everyone was walking on eggshells. As my daughter Leanne made plans for Australia, there was no doubt in my mind that she couldn't wait to get out of her hellish family life.

That fall, after Denise went back to school, she shared with me that she ate her lunch in the cubicle of the washroom because she didn't want anyone to see her eating anything. This broke my heart, knowing that this was how she was coping at school; and from that point on, I made it my job to pick her up at lunch and take her back for the afternoon. You can imagine that as a mother, I wanted to keep her home and not have her faced with the anxiety of lunchtime. I was sick thinking this was how Denise was living her life; she was trapped inside a world where the eating disorder was taking complete control in her thoughts and actions. As a family, we too were trapped, trapped in the world of ED from the outside. There were many people telling me, "Just make her eat!" I had one well-meaning relative suggest for us to send her to them, and they would make her eat. This disorder was so misunderstood by most of our family and friends that it was easier for them to keep a distance. I know that they were afraid to talk about Denise, as they really had no idea what to say or do. As a family, we were very much alone and very frightened of the future.

Leanne left for her trip to Australia, which she had been planning for many months in November, and we had an extremely teary good-bye at the airport. Saying good-bye to Leanne was especially hard, as I knew that she had had enough living with a sister with an eating disorder; she didn't really understand what was happening and how Denise could not be getting any better. *Is Denise going to be okay? Will she survive the eating disorder, or will the eating disorder kill her?* This was the worst fear for all of us, although we never discussed it at that time. Through one of Leanne's close friends, we learned of a girl with an ED that didn't make it. This became more of a reality and instilled the fear in us all even more.

As the weeks passed, the ED really started to overwhelm Denise, and she ultimately became too sick to attend school. Her dance was also put on hold . . . yet this was what she loved and lived for, and although she kept in contact with a few of the girls, she truly missed not being able to dance. Faced with the reality of the eating disorder, we knew she was on the "downward spiral" that the psychotherapist had talked about. I would go to bed many nights crying. My husband was also scared but found it so difficult to share his feelings. Ross, her father, being a typical male, had never had to express his deep feelings and emotions. At this point, we would do almost anything to have our happy, sweet Denise back. Who was this girl? This was not Denise; it was someone else within her. We knew of no support groups to attend; it was just the family doctor, who really was of no use at all. If Denise was in the hospital program, we could tap into a support group, but this was not an option for us. I had no friends going through this. So we were really on our own, trying to explain to people that *we can't just make her eat*, as it was much more complicated than that. Our daughter Tanis was trying to deal with this as best as she could, yet I know she also was suffering. She also felt helpless and unable to reach Denise. There was a very thick wall that had been built around Denise, and all her loving family and friends were on the outside trying to be let in, but the ED would not have anyone in his world with Denise.

Six months from the first official visit to treat Denise's ED, we received a call from the children's hospital with an appointment for an assessment. We were relieved as her much-compromised health was finally going to be addressed by a team of experts. It was a very long day for Denise; and at the end of the day, my husband, daughter Tanis, and I were asked to join the assessment team for a meeting. It was suggested that Denise be admitted immediately. However, this was a problem, as there were only three beds designated for ED; and they were full. We were devastated. *How can they not admit her now, today, if she is so sick?* This was part of the waiting game—telling the parent, "Your child needs a bed, but take a number." Meanwhile, we better hope no other child comes in sicker because she would then get bumped and wait even longer. It was determined that until a bed became available, it would be best for Denise to stay at home and come in once a week to be monitored.

Denise became very depressed during this time, and it was clear that she was isolating herself from her friends and family; she was only comfortable around us and a couple close friends. Eventually, she trusted only a select few, including her boyfriend, my husband, her sister, and me. Family celebrations and holidays were a struggle, and Denise would find an excuse to not attend, as she seemed to struggle with large gatherings. These gatherings were also difficult for most of our extended family members who really didn't understand what she was going through. The majority of the family didn't know how to talk to Denise; they were afraid to call. I guess they couldn't find the words to express their love for her. Yes, we felt terribly isolated, coming from a large family of more than twenty close family members of grandparents, aunts, and uncles.

It was a very dark time in our life. I was sad that our extended family couldn't understand the seriousness, sadness, and loneliness of ED. I wondered whether there was a feeling of people silently questioning how I could let me daughter get so sick. Why didn't I stop her? Why did I let this happen to her? If I had the answers to these questions, I guess there wouldn't be a need for me to be writing this story.

Denise loved to help me shop for groceries and prepare meals but would not join us at the table. Her excuse was she had been nibbling and picking and was not hungry. I discovered later that this was the way she could control not having to join us and was a convenient way to skip meals. Another way to skip meals was to sleep through the morning so that by the time she was up, it was lunchtime. It was in discussing these traits with other parents' years later that we realized this was a very common practice. Naively, I believed that this was okay, as she wasn't burning any real calories in bed and she needed her rest. I also supposed the sleepiness was a side effect of her antidepressant medication.

A past acquaintance of mine through school was interviewed on the radio on a Sunday evening; it was odd for us to be listening to the radio at that time of day, but fate would have us tuned in. This was timely, as Cindy was being interviewed about the process her daughter had gone through with her eating disorder (ED), explaining the difficulty they went through with the medical system. I called her the next day and was told, "Get in the medical system now. Don't waste any time. Get in the system . . . take a number . . ." Was I buying a pair of shoes? No, I was trying to get prompt medical attention for my seriously ill child and wait in line for her number to be called. I was also warned that if your daughter tells you the treatment is not helping, don't hesitate to look elsewhere. Although this advice took me by surprise, I stored it in the back of my mind. Unfortunately, many doctors are not given much training about ED, which is part of the problem of not getting good initial care.

I took Denise shopping for some new clothes, as the wardrobe she once had was far too large; and since she had a few days prior to being admitted to the children's hospital, we decided to find some better-fitting clothes. Denise had lost so much weight, and I was horrified to be shopping in the children's department at the Gap for her new size! Other mothers shopping stared at us and probably wondered what was wrong with Denise, as she obviously was too tall to be shopping in this department of the Gap and was a frightening walking skeleton. We hadn't shopped at this store for years, and although the clothing suited her tall frame, they were too baggy on her. I could have cried on the spot!

On December 12, 2000, Denise was admitted to the children's hospital; we were so happy, thinking *how lucky we were to finally get the bed Denise so badly needed*. A few weeks went by, and there was a slight improvement. She seemed to be buying into the treatment. I wrote a poem thinking of Denise, hoping it would give her the encouragement and strength to recover:

Dear Denise

Just for today, do it for you.
We know you can, and will, beat this cruel dragon.

Attempting to understand the fear and anxiety you are going
through has been painful and heartbreaking for us as well as you.
We are encouraged and comforted knowing that help is here for
you today.

Our thoughts and prayers will be with you each day as you
explore and grow.

Remember we are here for you. To support and see you through
this difficult and challenging time.
You've got what it takes to break loose reunite with your
healthy mind and healthy body.

Make each day of recovery a stepping stone toward your
independence, freedom, and wellness.

We will do whatever it takes to help you close this very
frightening chapter in your life.

With everlasting love to you always,

Hugs and kisses, Mom and Dad
XOXO

As they say, "the honeymoon was over"; and after seven weeks, we realized that Denise wanted to get better, but the treatment was not adequate. She was so desperate to get better, so desperate that while sitting idle in the hospital, Denise researched many treatment facilities worldwide and pleaded for us to send her somewhere to get her the treatment she so desperately needed. Denise knew there was more to this disease and, with great insight, stated, "Eating more food is not going to fix the problem. I really want to get better, but I need more therapy."

It was such a shame that so much valuable time had been lost, and she was so motivated to get better. In an emergency visit with her psychiatrist, my husband and I were told that Denise was planning to run away from the hospital with another patient who also was not responding well to treatment. We were shocked and knew time was of the essence to make a fast change. The fear of having her run away from the hospital was very real, as we knew that others in the past had been successfully in escaping. I use the word "escape" because this is the best word to express the angst the girls were living with. Ross and I drove home from the hospital fretful and hoping that Denise would be there in the morning. I cried myself to sleep, at a loss as to how this could happen . . . I blamed myself for Denise being so ill. I again questioned myself as to how this happened and why I didn't see it coming or stop it before it became so serious. This was such a horribly painful time as a mother . . . I was blaming myself and living in terror with no one to turn to.

I remember that when Denise was first admitted to the hospital, we were not allowed to take her outside for fresh air. At week five, permission was given to take Denise outside for some fresh air and a walk. She was allowed to go as long as she stayed in her wheelchair, and when she finally was outside, we were dismayed to find that the natural light hurt her eyes! We knew that it had been far too long since she had been exposed to sunlight, but the "special team" working with Denise did not see any problem keeping her in the hospital without fresh air and sunshine. This was truly shocking to us. Why would the hospital staff deprive Denise of this essential link to wellness? I was very fortunate to have my dear friend Cindy as my main support and sense of hope. Cindy's daughter had been to a treatment center a year previous, and she was able to provide me with much-needed support. During Denise's hospitalization, Cindy helped me understand how important it was to get Denise promptly into an intensive treatment place for recovery.

The next few days were spent on the phone interviewing people from eating disorder centers. They all gave us the hope we so desired and considered necessary for Denise. This was especially true of the people at Remuda Ranch in Arizona, who really seemed to care about our daughter. Suddenly, we were filled with excitement, sensing this was the treatment that would work for Denise! The children's hospital did not try to stop us from discharging our dangerously ill child.

We had a very short lead time to make the arrangements for Denise; we couldn't wait for the government to okay and cover the cost of this out-of-country treatment. We knew getting the help for Denise needed to be expedited, and it was our responsibility as any concerned parent longing for the best possible care for their child. The next day, Denise had an in-depth telephone interview with the intake nurse at Remuda; this was followed by an interview with my husband and me. We then had to wait a couple days before they had an opening. I went to the children's hospital, filled out the discharge papers, and brought Denise home. We never had contact with the children's hospital from this point on, not even a follow-up call to ask how Denise was doing. It is really quite shocking considering this was a patient treated not for just seven hours, but for seven weeks.

Many tears flowed throughout the family leading up to the day when Denise and I were leaving for Arizona. Our family was comforted knowing this was the direction required for the recovery from this insidious disease. The house tension was released, and feelings of relief were just around the corner. Our flights were booked, and arrangements were made for the rental car I would need after I registered Denise and said good-bye. The staff at Remuda stipulated the types of clothes that were allowed and made it clear that no cell phones or electronics were permitted. We had never been to Arizona; and this journey was therefore filled with feelings of optimism, encouragement, and apprehension concerning the outcome of Denise's recovery. Denise was ready for the intensive weeks and hard work ahead; she was a bundle of nerves and was very anxious, but there was also a sense of calm within her. She slept for most of the flight, and I stroked her hair, which is something she loved as a small child. My lap was a pillow for her. I cherished the time we had left before I would give her the last hug and kiss for a long time. I had mixed feelings during the flight as I was so apprehensive. *Am I doing the right thing?* My internal dialogue always affirmed that this was best for Denise.

On arrival to Remuda, we were led into an office and introduced to the nurse who would be part of Denise's team. We had only a couple of minutes to be together. I hugged Denise's frail body tightly. We didn't want to separate, but we also sensed a sincere love and trust at this place. With one last hug, Denise was promptly taken away, and that was the last I would see of her for a long time. Although I didn't want to leave her, I left feeling more hope than I had experienced in a long time. This insidious disease was going be treated by a professional treatment team that was highly regarded for excellent adolescent care and had the statistics to prove its good ratings.

This was one of most frightening times as a parent with a child so sick—having nowhere to turn in Canada, but to have to go to the United States for the care she deserved and needed immediately. Denise was so thin that her bones were visible everywhere. She was a walking skeleton and was dressed in many layers not only because of the loss of body temperature, but also to hide her skeleton. Her hair was thinning and falling out; the hair on her arms was thickening to help insulate and keep her warmer. She was so dauntingly thin that there just wasn't much left to her. I prayed over and over for the wisdom of the new treatment team to help them understand why Denise was so ill and how they could help her into recovery. I also prayed for our family to have the strength and faith we needed for this challenging time. We regret wasting important healing time in our city in Canada. The re-feeding was imperative, but the lack of valid supportive psychotherapy was inexcusable. I still find it hard to accept that this is how we are willing to treat our sick young children. They all have bright futures ahead until an ED strikes. Why is it so difficult to understand that the outcomes are far greater with immediate help and care? As with any disease or illness, you have the best outcomes with prompt attention and treatment. Leaving your homeland and venturing into another country to get help for your child is uncalled for and unacceptable. We are not the only family; there had been many before us and many after us having to sacrifice so much to get the help that their child deserves.

The first week in treatment at Remuda, we had no contact with our daughter, but we could send her faxes to let her know how much we loved and missed her. We were worried and wondered how Denise was doing, yet we had full confidence in the people treating Denise. I returned home feeling that she would be well cared for and treated with respect. I had faith that she would be cherished as she should be. As each day passed, the worry lessened, and we felt more confident knowing Denise was in good hands. Denise earned telephone time, and we were scheduled for weekly family therapy sessions over the phone. Progress was evident, and our very sick daughter was slowly showing signs of improvement! During her first week, a nasal feeding tube was recommended to help with the re-feeding. Denise was in agreement, and we authorized this treatment. Within a few weeks, Denise was offered an activity challenge on the high ropes . . . funny how she wasn't well enough to even go for a walk while at the children's hospital! She took the challenge and willingly gave up some control, put her trust in others, and successfully completed the challenge! Wow, we were thrilled with the change in her! Each phone call and therapy session showed improvement. Denise was thinking more clearly and was so much happier; we were overjoyed to see the change in such a short period of time. It was six weeks since Denise left for treatment, and as part of the treatment, our whole family was required to participate in a one-week family therapy session. We, therefore, booked a flight for our eldest daughter, who was still traveling, to be present with the family. It was a very spiritual week of healing at Remuda called "truth and love." This was a life-altering week for all of the families involved. If only every family could participate in a week of therapy before any real problems surface, it would benefit them for a lifetime.

Two weeks later, we began arranging the aftercare, which is essential to have in place prior to the discharge. We recognized that there was going to be a lack of qualified people back home for

Denise, and therefore, we decided to look elsewhere for support. We had an opportunity to meet with a therapist named Christina, who was located in the Okanagan Valley. We thought this would be the ideal place to relocate, as this therapist was empathetic and really understood ED! Denise and I moved to the Okanagan in order for her to receive follow-up care. My husband was able to work close by half of the time, and my daughter Tanis stayed home as she was attending college. This was a challenge at times, as I missed time with Tanis. I was able to go back home for a few days here and there, but I spent most of the time with Denise.

Denise worked with Christina for a few years; and we firmly believe she was an important key to her care, as it was at this time that she developed bulimia, which was a whole new experience and education for our family. The bulimia started when Denise was more confident and began enjoying food again. She had a job at a local bread garden and was frequently assigned the closing hours. With access to lots of food and permission to bring home whatever bake goods were left over at the end of the day, she began to binge. At first, I had no idea what was happening, and I was just happy to see her eating again. When I realized this was out of control, I was extremely frightened and cried thinking this was the beginning of something really ugly. We were very scared and distressed. Christina was so helpful explaining the traits and changes of the person with bulimia; they had no regard for the property of others. Denise's sisters knew all about this, as they discovered they couldn't trust her with their clothes, makeup, and other personal effects. It was long before Denise's eating disorder that Leanne and Tanis bought locks for their bedroom doors. Growing distrust and hate developed between Denise and her sisters, when they once were so close and loving. Utilizing the tools developed at Remuda and counseling with Christina, Denise was able to gradually change the behaviors and overcome the bulimia. After about three years, our family supported Denise's decision to stop the therapy because she felt that continuing to talk about the ED was going to make it impossible to let go.

I suggested she see a Chinese medicine doctor, who gave her herbs and acupuncture a few times a week. It was then we could really see her coming around once again. A couple years ago, Denise wanted to use a personal trainer to help her get back on to a healthier workout routine, and she has found this trainer also to be part of the missing puzzle. The trainer herself had been afflicted with an ED years before and completely understood how Denise was feeling. She was her confidant and mentor.

The past few years, we have noticed an exhilarating return of our daughter; she is now at college, working part-time, and has developed a successful business of makeup artistry on the side. Denise's life is more balanced, and she is very happy. She moved out a year ago with her sister Tanis for the first time. She has the skills, ambition, and desire to succeed; and we know she will. Just recently, their lease was up, and Denise has moved back home but is still working hard to finish her schooling and working part-time. We love having her home again but know this won't last for long before she decides to travel a little. It's wonderful to see the excitement and zest of life back in her eyes; we are truly grateful!

There were many struggles along the way during the aftercare, but we are now breathing easier knowing we did what was needed to save our daughter. Our only regret, after going through this ten-year journey, was not getting the essential help Denise needed in a timely manner. Waiting with your name on lists and availability of beds should not dictate how a child is treated. This is a mental illness and has the highest mortality rate, and therefore, I can't help but wonder if we would leave a child with cancer to wait so long for treatment. Of course not, the system is broken, and we are waiting till our youth are gravely medically compromised before it is taken seriously.

What helped me get through this traumatic time was my lifeline with close family and friends. There weren't many people to confide in that had experienced having a child with an ED. Looking back to the first doctor we saw, he really didn't have a clue nor did the last one Denise saw before she went into the hospital. It was a few years into Denise's journey with ED before our doctor would ask me what

I knew about this disorder in order to help with her patients. It is a sad fact and completely absurd that doctors are asking the patients' mothers to educate them.

I have my life back too! During this horrific time in my life, I joined forces with two other moms who also have been through the journey of having a very sick daughter with an ED. We met in 2002 and asked ourselves why it was that we sent our children far away to another country to give them the care they needed and deserved. As a result, we formed the nonprofit group called the Looking Glass Foundation for Eating Disorders. We have recently opened Canada's first intensive treatment facility for adolescents suffering with eating disorders. We have been organizing fund-raisers since inception and will require many more years of fund-raising. We have worked tirelessly with the government and communities to make this a reality. We have also had a summer camp for adolescents to help them and also give respite to the families for a week. Some communities have contacted us to help raise awareness and do fund-raisers, which really makes it all well worth the time and effort we have been volunteering for the past seven years. We launched an ad campaign to raise awareness throughout British Columbia, Canada, and it was shown nationally. Looking Glass continues to have good relationships with the international professionals in the world of ED. We have purchased the facility on lovely nine-acre site on Galiano Island in British Columbia, Canada, which is a very healing and nurturing setting away from the city and all its distractions.

I still take many calls from desperate parents who are caught in the confusing world of eating disorders. Each child goes through many different experiences, and unfortunately, most don't get the immediate help and care they need. Without proper care and treatment, these children struggle for many years, and some don't survive. My heart goes out to the families of those who died. I am so thankful that we have been able to give hope and faith to those that are on this journey with their loved ones. Having an intensive treatment team scheduled early at the onset of an ED increases the chance of survival.

I wish for all families to not doubt what is going on with your child. Don't think that your child won't get really sick; be the advocate of your child's needs. Don't be afraid to second-guess the doctors and professionals, as some of them are just learning about this disorder too. There is a small window of opportunity to get the treatment needed before the brain becomes impaired, so you must act swiftly. As parents, we do our best to be practical, sensitive, and loving to our child's body, mind, and soul; therefore, we must release the parental guilt we carry around, as it can be all consuming—a worried parent's heart is heavy enough. We need to find the faith within to have the hope for recovery for our child. We are thrilled to have our Denise back! She now is accepting of who she is and realizes we all love her just the way she is. Most importantly, don't be afraid to pray and ask God for direction and comfort. God will listen to those who ask.

Why am I discouraged? Why is my heart so sad?
I will put my hope in God-I will praise him again
My Savior and my God!

—Psalms 42:11

Chapter Six

This Too Shall Pass
Ruth Dubois

I saw some signs. I wondered if something was wrong. But I needed Denise to be strong and healthy because it fit with my own expectations of self as the perfect mother, the knowledgeable nursing instructor, the together woman, the grounded master's student, and so on. Thus, whenever I thought I saw something unusual, a little voice would butt in, *Let's not be dramatic here. No need to overreact. No daughter of mine could be anorexic! She's just being a teenager. This too shall pass.*

But what I noticed was not going away, was not just my imagination, and was not making me very comfortable—things like little notes on the kitchen counter itemizing her food intake by how many bites of food she had eaten, interspersed with the word "purged." *Purged.* What thirteen-year-old even knows that word? She refused to eat anything that messed up the plate—rice, salad, casseroles, pasta. If I really thought about it, there were not many foods on the list that were acceptable to her anymore. There was the Easter weekend, where she read a novel all the way to my sister-in-law's about a person with an eating disorder. And then there was the time when her father found her chewed food in a napkin or stuffed along the underside of her plate and evidence of purging in the downstairs toilet. Lots of little things at first, but none of them on their own seemed cause for real concern. I kept telling myself, *She's okay. She is just missing her older sister. She's okay. Lots of high school girls are focused on their weight. She's okay. Look at all her waiflike friends. She's okay. Look how active she is on the soccer field . . . She's okay.*

Gradually, insidiously, there came a day when she was not okay; and I could no longer quell my inner voice. Her best friend told the school counselor at about the same time our Rotary Exchange student confided to me that she was very worried about Denise. It seemed to all come crashing down at once. My perfectly normal world fell apart, as I realized that my beautiful, accomplished thirteen-year-old daughter was in serious trouble . . . losing weight at an alarming rate and becoming more and more secretive. The school was calling all too often those days to report her fainting episodes and informing me of the counselor's decision to take Denise to the family physician without allowing me to be present. So now my inner voice beseeched me to not let anyone know. *You can handle this calmly! This is a family matter. It will upset her sister, so best not to tell her. Denise just needs reassurance and some boundaries.*

Trying to keep it all inside was driving me crazy. It has never been my nature to suppress my emotions and thoughts. I desperately needed a confidante, or maybe several, to listen, to accept, and to give me strength—but not to judge or to give pat answers. Yet I was ever mindful of the sensitive nature of this information and that we live in a very small community, where people's affairs are never private for very long. I was very afraid for Denise and did not want to do anything to make her life more challenging or to send her further away than I already sensed she was feeling.

It was not long before I was unable to keep the secret. A friend remarked in church about how "gorgeous" Denise was becoming; but what she was really seeing were the big doe like eyes in a lean face, the jutting hip bones and collarbones in a skeletal frame, a transparency to her skin accentuating a frailty I had never seen before. The mother of one of Denise's soccer friends commented at a game that she had heard Denise was anorexic and advised me to set some ground rules, such as no going out with friends until she ate her three meals a day. It was getting around our small community. I was the mother of the girl with an eating disorder. Now my inner voice intoned, *People think it's your fault . . . you are not the perfect mother . . . people with eating disorders have attachment problems with their mothers or—wait a minute, it's the other way 'round. People with eating disorders are over involved with their mothers . . . you must have done something wrong, and now you're losing her . . . she might even die!*

These catastrophic thoughts and panicky feelings ultimately drove me to insanity. As the fear and confusion roiled in my brain, I realized I needed to seek answers in the ways I had always solved problems. So I turned to books and read everything I could find about anorexia and eating disorders. I talked to every professional in my sphere about this mental illness and reverted to my take-charge, action-oriented self. I called eating disorder clinics, seeking information and confirmation that I had every right to advocate for help for Denise. I visited a friend who is a psychiatrist, and while his gloomy prognostications were not reassuring, I was further galvanized to seek help for Denise and our family. I remember taking myself in hand, asking myself, *What do I need right now?* I realized that to be supportive for Denise, I had to be grounded and healthy myself. There was no use in us both falling apart.

It was at this point that both my husband and I sought solace in each other and in our faith as Christians. I remember vividly the day that Denise had to be intubated with a feeding tube. We had been warned that her heart was showing signs of stress from the malnutrition and that her physician would elect to feed her by nasogastric tube if things got any worse. I arrived to the pediatrics floor to find my husband slouched disconsolately in a chair just outside the door to the unit. He had been told to leave her room so they could place the tube and had to listen to her crying and screaming during the procedure. His eyes were haunted and moist with unshed tears, and we melded together in misery at the thought of what had just taken place. Once home, I read him a chapter from *Reviving Ophelia*, by Mary Pipher, a book I was reading at the time about mothers and daughters with eating disorders. We both wept with some relief knowing that we were doing the best we could in difficult times. At one of our most terrible moments during Denise's illness, the phone rang, and people with whom we associated at the curling arena called to invite us to supper. They knew that we were going through a tough time and offered for us to go to a nearby pub and laugh a little. I remember we went out wondering if we would be any kind of fun and found ourselves laughing and talking about other things in life. It just felt so good and so normal.

I have always been a person who processes experiences by verbalizing and sharing ideas with others, so my initial inclination to keep this all a secret was in opposition to my past effective strategies for coping. I decided to share our struggles with a few key supporters in my life, and I told Denise that while she might not want me to reveal anything about our problems, I needed to seek support to get through them and to be there for her. Surprisingly, she was less worried about this decision than I had anticipated. Though she continued to deny that there was really any need for alarm, she did not plead with me to hide my own reactions. I chose to tell my sister everything I was feeling—the good, the bad, and the very ugly. She would phone often; but if I was feeling really isolated and lost, I knew I could always call her, and she would accept me wherever I was at. She listened well and rarely offered any advice. It just helped to say the words, to figure things out loud, and to know that she was there with sustaining faith that we would get through this troublesome time. When Denise was subsequently transferred to a psychiatric facility near my sister for further treatment, this special sister was there physically, visiting and staying with me on occasion in my room at Ronald McDonald House. I remember her as being calm, funny, reassuring, and accepting. She seemed sure that we would all survive this. Of course, there were many others who were also there in very tangible ways through the months, but I will forever remember my sister as my rock during that time.

I often argued with God in my head and sometimes out loud in my car as I drove home from work or the hospital. Strangely, He seemed ever so close in so many ways, yet so distant at the same time. I could not really find comfort in others' reassurances that

He held us in His hands, but I accepted with gratitude and some wonder the number of people who said they were praying for us. I recall that one friend sent word to her mother in England and later learned that her mother's prayer group kept us in their thoughts for months! My colleagues in my master's class kept a candle burning in the university campus during the summer of 2000 when they were studying there while I had to be absent because of Denise's hospitalization. Knowing that others were taking care of the praying parts let me concentrate on arguing, bargaining, and pleading with God. It was through these confrontations that I shouted out my pain, begged Him for some answers, and somehow found comfort. I remember playing a little game in my head as I would drive the six-kilometer stretch up our mountain road to home. I would count my blessings—no whining allowed for those few minutes. It was awesome how often I turned the corner to our street with a lighter heart and a brief feeling of release—just from that little exercise of positive thinking!

There were many times when I felt like our family was literally falling apart at the seams. Our eldest daughter, Teresa, was away that year on a school-exchange experience in Belgium; so she was physically separated when Denise's symptoms became manifest. We initially tried to keep it from her, as her own challenges in learning and living with another culture and language with strangers seemed daunting enough. Eventually, Denise shared her troubles with her sister, and Teresa did experience significant depression. In addition to missing her terribly, I was now also very worried because we could not support her well from so far away.

Contributing to this sense of family fracture was the reality that my husband worked and lived in another community, one and a half hours east of our home. He commuted weekly, and we had daily telephone contact; but nevertheless, I often felt very alone with our troubles. He sacrificed a lot to commute for family meetings and to consult with Denise's health care team during the weeks she was there. When Teresa returned home at about the same time Denise was finally discharged from hospital, we all drove home in one car, and I remember feeling a sense of relief that we were at last on a road to healing as one family unit. However, there were to be many challenges, as we reacquainted with one another in relationships seriously altered by our respective life experiences over that intense year. Teresa lent a supportive presence to her sister, which often transcended what I was able to offer in my motherly relationship with Denise, and I truly felt she brought stability and strength to our family. In some ways, I may have leaned on her too much as she made her own difficult transitions back into Canadian culture. To this day, these two sisters are reliant on each other in what has evolved to be a close connection of friendship and trust.

The crisis of anorexia shook our family for at least six months—from Denise's admission to a local pediatrics unit, to an adolescent psychiatric unit, and then, following her discharge, from facility to community care. During this time, she was re-nourished with nasogastric tube feedings, participated in behavioral and cognitive psychotherapy, and was prescribed drug therapy. We all participated in family therapy, as we tried to look at what needed to be reconciled in our personal relationships. There were many desperate moments and dark days along the way. Anorexia and other eating disorder problems are complex illnesses, frequently accompanied by other mental aberrations, including depression, substance abuse, self-mutilation, and conduct disorder. Drug therapy results in uncomfortable side effects, and the sequelae of purging often leads to abdominal discomfort and confused internal messages regarding hunger and satiety. The early months after her diagnosis and medical treatment were followed by years of a myriad of psychotherapeutic interventions, endless heartrending discussions, and copious tears—hers and mine.

As we shared our struggle with the social worker and other health professionals with whom we met during active treatment and subsequent to Denise's discharge from acute care, it often felt invasive and threatening. I blamed myself and my husband for somehow causing this problem, especially when I read in the literature about the risk factors for people developing eating disorders. It seemed that parenting factors and the family-of-origin issues were almost always implicated, so how could I not feel responsible? Yet I knew in my heart that there were no parents who loved their children more than we did and that we had developed capacity through previous challenges to surmount obstacles when we all worked together. I believed in the power of positive self-talk: You can't ferry up the river to rerun the rapids. The water under the bridge is passed. Stay the present course and focus on loving us through this . . .

While we had respect for the professionals who were caring for our family, it was tempered by the realization that they did not always know best what we should do or how our family should embrace Denise in what was really our family concern. I remember developing this insight in what was our final encounter with family counseling. The counselor asked each of us to describe the effects of Denise's illness on us personally. First, I spoke and then her father and then her sister. While I silently witnessed the obvious distress this was causing Denise, it was Teresa who responded by refusing to participate any further in the discussion. Her assertiveness and willingness to advocate from her heart for her sister astounded me. She was not as intimidated by the expertise of the counselors and instead listened to her instincts about what was best for Denise and our family. We left the meeting and invited Denise to share how that experience had affected her. It was a profound turning point in my mind since it illuminated the resilience of our family and the awesome strength we held in the face of suffering, challenge, and hardship. Never again would I abdicate to the professionals what was ours. We knew how to heal ourselves; we just needed to take the steps in that direction hand in hand, consulting with professionals from time to time for suggestions and ideas. For our family, this has worked well, and we have all grown in the process. By focusing on the resources of our family's health rather than on the cracks and fissures that are inevitable during stressful times, my earlier sense of isolation, failure, and hopelessness were ameliorated.

Through it all, I have continued to hold firm in my belief that love conquers all, that Denise has the power to master her challenges, and that *she* is not her disease. It is a feature of her being, but she is not defined by it. In the early days, when she would verbalize irrational thinking characteristic of a person with anorexia, I would tell her, "That is not you speaking, Denise. That is anorexia talking, and he needs to leave you and our home right now!" She thought it was I who was crazy, talking such nonsense, but I truly believe it was an important assertion of my belief that this phenomenon called anorexia did not define her and never should.

I have come to accept that Denise's eating disorder is not an acute disease with a self-limiting end. It continues to present challenges in her life, sometimes more compellingly than at other times, and requires her to employ a variety of coping strategies and supports. It has been ten years now; and she has matured into an insightful, empathic, beautiful young woman—enjoying her career and a fulfilling relationship with a young man who is now walking this journey of healing with her. While I never anticipated the agony of watching my precious daughter suffer as she had, I now marvel at the incredible growth in our mother-daughter relationship, as well as in the resilience and strength of our family. I know she may continue to face other trials related to what is now more characteristic of bulimia, but I feel sure she is empowered by the strengths she has cultivated. I am more or less at peace about it.

Come quickly to help me, O Lord my savior.
                                    —Psalms 38:22

Chapter Seven

A Daughter's Story: Mami, Can You Hear Me?
Denise Palacios

Mother's love is peace. It need not be acquired, it need not be deserved.
                                    —Erich Fromm

TOILETS AND PAPER

My mother always kept the bathroom clean—as if she knew that this sacred place would be my sanctuary, a place I would long for, and a prison for my sanity and hope. The white tile floors became a most comfortable and refreshingly cool tomb, and the all-too-bright fluorescent white lighting that reflects on the floor creates a luminous ambiance for slow death. As I am embracing the toilet, curly hair pulled back, I stop and listen. Although I could suppress the noise of the gagging, every so often, I prayed that my mother would hear the vomit pour into the toilet bowl and save me from the monstrous disease that was killing me, destroying me, slowly but quite surely. I feel bulimia is to my body as writing is to my soul. I vomit every imaginable stress into something white. To *vomit* can suggest the actual purging after consuming massive amounts of foods, or it means the purging of frightening thoughts onto paper. White is pertinent to my salvation. Three years ago, New Year's 2008, the white beacon I was consumed with took the shape of a gleaming white porcelain toilet. I later lovingly refer

67

to the toilet with my therapist as "the Monster." The structure of the toilet became an illicit lover I would frequently embrace and collapse into, and my lover was always there, waiting for me—with tender arms and a soothing touch. Conveniently, there was a mirror placed directly beside the toilet. After the hours spent vomiting my sins into this maddening bowl, I would stare at my round face, with black rivers rolling down the plains of my still-rosy cheeks.

The first time I see my eyes bleed is the second time I throw up. My large eyes, chocolate almonds adorning the whiteness of the sclera, were now filled with little pools of blood, placid lakes that restrain the salt water. This lake was haunted with high tides of the joy that came with the overindulgence of food and low tides of miserable desperation because of their disposal. The moment when these two tides would cross paths is when the blood of my disease was born, between the misery and joy that comes with bulimia.

After the painful thrusting of my small fingers into my throat, the ambitious wave of the heaving controls my body, and I prepare for the torment I am about to put my body through again. The acid rumbles and erupts in my stomach like a vicious volcano. It bursts through my esophagus with relentless rage—burning me, incinerating my insides and my spirit, creating ashes of my distant and dying dreams. The vomit victoriously reaches my mouth and explodes into the bowl, destroying the pristine toilet water. As if I had just run an epic marathon, I feel proficient and proud. I peer over the rim of the toilet and gaze at the vomit that I refuse to flush down immediately. I want to *see* the vomit because it feels like an exhausting triumph. This vomit means so much to me. I could kiss, stroke, hold it close to my cheek, feel it between my fingers, adore, and despise. I feel pride because the sickening redemption of torturing my body qualifies me to live another day. I am unshackled of my errors for that moment. Every sin I committed is absolved; every wrong is right. Most importantly, every pound of waste is no longer inside of my body.

Throwing up adds another day to my life and takes another one away; however, I do not know this yet. I am too consumed with consuming and disposing. With the blinding white light above me, a spotlight illuminates my disease, and I am exposed only to myself and the frightened reflection to my right. I muster up enough bravery to glance at this frightened girl—this girl that was once my mother's baby, the youngest of the family, the little one with the large eyes, cheeks, and curls. The glance imprisons my interest, and I look into her deep yet shallow eyes. These eyes that once screamed one million heartaches and overflowed overwhelming agonies now appeared so vacant, lonely, and dead. I stared at my face, struggling to breathe, remembering why I am doing this. I get distraught and horrified by the destruction I am causing my body. After I purge everything—the four tuna sandwiches with much mayonnaise, a gallon of fruit punch, a large bag of sour cream and onion chips, chocolate cookies, and one more tuna sandwich—I see the pink pulpous mass that lies at the bottom of the bowl, as my dreams of a peaceful life lie at the bottom of an ocean.

Mami, I wish you could peel me off the bathroom floor, wipe the matted hair off my moist forehead, and put your tiny cool hand on my searing neck. I wish I could fall into your arms, instead of falling into this wretched toilet. Soothe me, Mami, let me fall apart near your heart.

The year is 2008. I throw up every day, at least four times a day for this year. This is the year when one drunken December night, I deliciously contemplated taking my life. It was past midnight and before 3:00 a.m., I am not sure. Time does not matter when you are drowned in alcohol and thoughts of suicide. I had run out of canvas to paint on, and the pure white bedroom walls before me seemed like the practical surface to use. I picked up the paintbrush, and my hand furiously trembled as I made my way toward the white and watched in horror as the words purged onto the wall . . . there were the words of hatred for a young woman who was desperate to exist. A frenzy began, and I could not control where my arm was going, what words went where. I paint words like "fat" and "coward," trembling fetuses and hearts. In Spanish, I write, "Ya no te quiero." I collapsed on my bedroom floor and cried for hours, hating myself for being fat, hating the cruel monstrous vomit that tricked me into believing it could make me beautiful. I hated myself for being ungrateful and destructive. Curled up on the frigid floor, I feel the draft of the winter wind cool my scorching sorrow. I glanced back to the wall. At the bottom, I had written, "God, help me find my way."

I remembered my mother and her small hands. I dreamt of the violet sky as the wind whispered on. I want to stay. I want to live . . .

A quiet promise was made to God. I vowed to stop throwing up and love myself the way He loved me because I deserved to understand why I became bulimic. I was pushed to the jagged edge of desperation, where it was so simple to fall off and forget all the blessings that were flushed away with all the food. My darling mother, who only lived to comfort me, was waiting for my return—away from that desolate edge, where I prayed for a draft to push me over. Instead of sending the wind, God smiled on my life and led me out of the dark.

And so I began to write. I write for days, and I cannot stop. I do not stop. I found that my beloved sheets of paper and roughly smooth canvas were now the white beacons to mend my maladies—a white canvas to spill my wounds into, to vomit the words I could never say. I write of the things that break my heart. I write of my aborted children. I write of nothing. I write of everything. I often found streams of my naked tears creating blue rivers on the white sheets, turning them into raw relics of hope. I finally write of hope. Hope was the innocent quality of my damaged spirit that was muddled with the muddy vomit that would devour my life. After the vomit, I found my beauty. I found that the things I would write became gorgeous thoughts of an ugly disease. I discovered what I want to do. I yearn to transform the grotesque into the beautiful, to shed light on the damp and dreary alleyways my mind always lingers on. Something was birthed from my damaged body. Like a comet that begins with a fiery fury and later leaves remnants of stars that spray across the sky and illuminate the darkest of dreams, I discovered on the white sheets that the vomit made me beautiful. Fat people don't find love.

No one will ever marry you if you're fat. These words sing to me with an aching and menacing bravado that has replayed as an overwhelming orchestra for eighteen years. I hear it when I get dressed, before I step into the shower, when I would pinch my waist with the hopes of making the slabs of fat evaporate. There, I am a beautiful and slender girl. It took me those years to understand that this was a lie from my dearest father, one he utilized as a precaution so that I do not become obese. Obesity is my father's worst enemy. An obese person represents everything he hates: lazy, unattractive, degenerate, pathetic, egotistical, and dirty. My father has worked in the fields of the Ecuadorian farms he was raised in since he was five. He knows how difficult it is to earn your daily bread, and he finds people who abuse that bread are disgusting and repulsive. And I love me some bread.

In the winter of 1992, my mother, father, and sister sit at the dinner table. I am five. My father's sweat and tenacity bleeds through the walls of our three-family house in Newark, New Jersey. My neighborhood is gritty to some, pretty to me. We live a block away from my Catholic school, around the corner from the library, where I would spend hours hiding in books. Our second-floor apartment is quaint and lovely, with lots of windows that saturate the house with sun or the gloom of gray days. Dinner is at seven, always, and I have a steaming plate of spaghetti in front of me. I happily devour every succulent strand of the grainy starch, savoring the taste of the drenched pasta, and lick my fingers clean of the gravy that has spilled through them. My lips are stained with gravy, as are my cheeks and my white shirt. (Mami always reminds me, after we have spaghetti, to wear a bib or something dark.) I smile because food has always made me happy. It is a Saturday night, and we watch the program of the evening while we eat: *Sabado Gigante con Don Francisco!* There is a marriage segment on the show, where men propose to women and have a live quickie marriage in front of millions of families, watching with shallow, bated breaths, like mine.

As I do every night, I finish my dinner and skip to my father's seat. He is seated at the head of the table, looking like a dictator, with his shoulders back, hands crossed, inspecting everything. I climb on his lap, with the five-year-old hope of connecting with this man whom I constantly fear, hope of embracing the sadness in his eyes, and hope of him letting me have a sip of his Coca-Cola on ice. I stroke his black hair, with stripes of silver peeking through, curly and thick. His cheek is stubby after a long days' work, and I love the way it feels. He lets me sit and shakes his knee, so I hop up and down as we watch a young couple, maybe in their thirties, quickly get dressed for their public ceremony. I say, "I would never get married on TV." I do not know why I say that. I always resided comfortably in my private inner self, underneath the safety of a stoic pretense, observing everything and saying nothing, brown eyes wide. I am still hopping up and down on his knee, and he pats my tummy filled with pasta and says, "No one will ever marry you if you stay fat."

My childish smile immediately fades, fades into this incepted thought that would change my life to the lie that festered into my distorted image of what makes someone beautiful. I wish I never said what I said because as a five-year-old, I have provoked the foundation of the pains my father would consequently provide. I did not know that I would become a person that my father could hate, and I did not know that as I aged, I would work so hard to preserve that hatred. From this moment on, food becomes an illicit obsession, one that I will consequently use to defy my father's cruelty. But this night, I realize that I will never be beautiful, and I will always be certain of this for the next eighteen years.

*　　*　　*

The year is 2005, and Franco wakes up at 6:00 a.m. on the last Thursday of November. He takes the turkey out of the refrigerator and shoves it in the oven. We never know why he chooses to roast the turkey so early, and we never ask. We just become accustomed to Thanksgiving brunch. I sit on my father's left, as always, and I do not look him in the eye. His hair is now silver, and the same sadness of his hazel eyes have created bags of desolation and exhaustion underneath them. He is heavyset. His love of rice and true love of vodka have caused his body to expand. I am nineteen. Mary, underneath her glasses and a mass of curly hair and beauty marks, sits across from him; and they discuss politics and the importance of education. My mother, in her soft white dress and honey hair, is on his right, quick to bring him anything she might have forgotten. My father's fury had seized my mother's voice, even to defend her daughter. And then there is me, with a maroon attitude, hiding in my curly hair that has grown down to my waist, protecting my body from inspection.

He is my warden, carefully eyeing just how much salt I put in my soup, counting the bites I take, careful to notice my breathing, making sure I am eating *only* because I am hungry—not out of gluttony. I sense his peripheral stares, and my rage begins to rumble at his scrutiny. I feel exposed because my mother and sister know this is a touchy subject, and we all wait for the remarks he will make that will ignite the maddening fury that comes with sitting at the table. He makes remarks like "*Versa* (You'll see)," and "*Te segues engordando* (You stay fattening yourself up)." I am angry. I want to keep eating—and just because I know he doesn't want me to. I want to throw my plate across his face and bury my food into his mouth. I do neither. I just keep eating. I keep glaring at my food that is so delicious and begs me to eat it. Food will never tell me no, unlike my father. I roll my eyes, grit my jaw, and say nothing.

I shuffle my five-year-old self back to my place at the dinner table after I am humiliated. I say nothing. I wonder if he is right, if what he says is true, like Santa Claus or the Easter bunny. As I sit back down in my chair to his left, I let my curly bangs cover my eyes, amid my curly afro that my mother keeps cutting, so that my father does not see that he has punctured my heart. No one sees it. He has succeeded in allowing me to feel fat and discouraged the possibility that anyone would ever love me for my protruding tummy and chubby cheeks. He had begun to enforce his hate for obesity and the hate that I felt he had for me, his youngest child. My head is kept low so they do not see the dark clouds that form over my eyelids and over my soul and spirit nor the idle waves spilling and sloshing between my lashes. An imminent storm begins to brew, forming precipitation to slowly wash my self-esteem away. No one sees me cry.

* * *

I have not thrown up in 807 days. When I eat too much bread or have too much ice cream, I am reminded of the urge to throw up. When I burp up the air of a pizza, with the memory of the acidic gravy and cheese, I burn, scald, and tear my throat. I remember the vomit each time I go into my bathroom and sit on the vessel that flushes away my dignity. When I drink too much Manischewitz wine and feel the miserable wave of nausea the next day, I think of politely shoving my index finger down my throat to dispose of the ghastly queasiness. I recall my disease when I glance at the same mirror I used to, right of the toilet, but see a different face looking at me with loving eyes.

My face is different; it glows . . .

It is as if I have left a place where I feared for my life, numbered my days, lived without sun—another country, I have no desire to return. This is a place without music—without the heavenly timbre of Maria Callas, the electric guitar of Jimi Hendrix, the audacity of Radiohead, the ominous and haunting keys of Rachmaninoff. A place without instruments like guitars, cymbals, keyboards. A country without Picasso, Van Gogh, or Chuck Close. Air without fragrances like that of lilac, cinnamon, and apple pie. A place without playing in the fields or taking delicious baths with sweet pea oils and candlelight. Without the aroma of Chinese rice with carrots and string beans my partner cooks, so we can sit at our dinner table, and she'll ask me about my day. A kitchen where Justina, with her hands on my waist from behind me as I wash the dishes, would whisper she adores me. It would not exist. That was a place without writing, without the ability to understand myself. A life deprived of my mother's sincere tenderness or her fragrant embrace. The marina of this place did not have ships so that I could not find other shores of tranquility. I would stand on that edge of the dock—or the edge of madness—and gaze at the immeasurable ocean and envision the dreams I could never conceive. No dreams. I could never go back to that place.

I was born again because I was dead, as dead as my eyes seemed when I stared into that mirror and found an ugly girl in the reflection, wiping the vomit from her lips. I miss that dead girl. When I evoke our shared anguish, I feel a throbbing in my chest. I have long grieved her and think of her only as a distant memory. I am the only person who knows where to find this lost girl. But I am afraid to look for her. When I look closely into my muddy eyes, I see her bending over that toilet. I want to peel her off the floor. I want to embrace her, stroke her massive hair, kiss her salty cheeks, and tell her how lovely she is, as I knew *Mami* would have if I only shared this aching secret with her.

As I write, my ghost visits me; and I visit her, softly wading through the rivers of her hopeless mind. This girl will always be inside of me. Because of her, I have sought other oceans and swam in other seas. For that, I cherish her and my mother more than I could another life. It is because of her; it is for her that I write this story.

Take delight in the Lord, and he will give you your heart's desires.

—Psalms 37:4

Afterword

It has been over five years since Melody attended the recovery center, but it hasn't been all sunshine and roses. There have been moments when Melody was sick or didn't eat a full meal, where the old familiar feelings of fear and panic have crept in and sent me to my knees in prayer. Fortunately, these feelings have lessened with each passing year, as she has shown her strength and healing when dealing with major issues and challenges. Melody thrived beautifully during the planning and preparation of her wedding, as well as the recent move with her new husband to a city far away from our family. She is comfortable with herself and her life and is looking forward to starting a family of her own, and I am learning to trust that she can take care of herself.

I have had time to reflect on our experience and consider what I could have done differently. Was I the cause of Melody's disorder because I was too busy working to notice her anxiety and struggles? Was it pride or fear that drove me to isolate from the help and support and try instead to "fix" her myself? After some thoughtful self-reflection, I discovered that eating disorders flourish in deceptive and manipulating environments. They are based on fear and lies; and we can drown in the swirl of anguish, guilt, anger, fear, and hopelessness if we are not vigilant. That is what happened. I sank like a rock, and it was only by the grace of God that I was able to swim back up to the surface, face this disease, and in turn help my daughter. This revelation caused me to ponder how other mothers survived this life-changing experience and what they learned along the way. These are the stories that comprise this book. So what did we learn? What can other mothers who have daughters battling an eating disorder gain from our experiences?

One of the biggest lessons learned is not to isolate. Repeated throughout the stories, mothers discovered that there were friends, family, and even colleagues who had been through this devastating experience either directly or by association. It is important to remember that there is hope, encouragement, and support available to sustain you through your daughter's struggle. The healing begins when you open up and share your fear and pain with people you trust. Isolation only feeds the feelings of anguish, guilt, fear, and hopelessness, which perpetuate the problem.

We also learned the lesson of self-care. Each of us spent so much time caring for our sick daughter and trying to hold our family together that we lost our sense of self. We became so absorbed in our daughter's illness that nothing else mattered except getting her well. Over a period of time, we stopped going out with friends and doing hobbies; and ultimately, we became depressed. We lost ourselves. The old saying "The hand that rocks the cradle rules the world" rings true. It is so vitally important that you get enough sleep, eat healthy meals, spend time with friends, and participate in enjoyable activities to maintain the emotional strength and energy needed to help your daughter and family.

Another lesson learned is to let go of the guilt. Eating disorders are a mental health issue, not the result of parenting mistakes. Eating disorders affect families of all demographics, religions, situations, and backgrounds in life. What we have in common is our love and determination in helping our daughter and doing the best we can. However, carrying the burden of assumed wrong decisions or wondering if we could have done things differently only impedes on the healing process. Give yourself permission to let the guilt go. You have moved heaven and earth for your daughter, and now you have to accept that there are some things you just can't fix. Allow the doctors and counselors to help your daughter while you continue to provide the much-needed emotional support.

And finally, we've learned to be educated about eating disorders. Recognizing the signs and symptoms is imperative in order to implement interventions as early as possible. Read books, talk to your doctor, attend support groups for parents, and read information on trusted websites. You cannot help your daughter if you don't understand the disorder or recognize the signs. The following pages provide a glossary of definitions and a comprehensive list of signs and symptoms for each of the eating disorders.

I pray that this book has provided you with hope, encouragement, and helpful information in seeking support for your daughter and family. I am eternally grateful to the mothers who were willing to share their private family pain in order to benefit mothers just beginning their journey. Have faith in God. He will sustain you through this difficult time.

Glossary

anorexia nervosa

An eating disorder characterized by a distorted body image, fear of becoming obese, persistent aversion to food, and severe weight loss and malnutrition. It most commonly affects teenage girls and young women.

bulimia nervosa

An eating disorder characterized by binge eating and compensatory behaviors like self-induced vomiting, excessive exercise, or misuse of laxatives to prevent weight gain.

compulsive overeating / binge eating disorder

An eating disorder characterized by *compulsive overeating* in which people consume huge amounts of food while feeling out of control and powerless to stop. It is often associated with obesity.

Signs and Symptoms of Eating Disorders

Anorexia nervosa/bulimia nervosa

From the www.something-fishy.org website:

- Dramatic weight loss in a short period of time
- Wearing big or baggy clothes or dressing in layers to hide body shape and/or weight loss
- Obsession with weight and complaining of weight problems
- Obsession with calories and fat content of foods
- Obsession with continuous exercise
- Frequent trips to the bathroom immediately following meals (with water running in the bathroom for a long period of time to hide the sound of vomiting)
- Visible food restriction / self-starvation
- Visible bingeing and/or purging
- Use or hiding use of diet pills, laxatives, or enemas
- Isolation, fear of eating around and with others
- Unusual food rituals like shifting the food around on the plate to look like it's been eaten, cutting food into tiny pieces, making sure the fork avoids contact with the lips, chewing food and spitting it out, dropping food into napkin on lap to throw away later
- Hiding food in strange places (closets, cabinets, suitcases, under the bed) to avoid eating (anorexia) or to eat at a later time (bulimia)
- Keeping a "food diary" or a list that consist of food and/or behaviors (e.g., purging, restricting, calories consumed, exercise, etc.)
- Loss of menstrual cycle

Compulsive overeating / binge eating disorder

- Fear of not being able to control eating and while eating not being able to stop
- Isolation, fear of eating around and with others
- Chronic dieting on a variety of popular diet plans
- Holding the belief that life will be better if they can lose weight
- Hiding food in strange places (e.g., closets, cabinets, suitcases, under the bed) to eat at a later time
- Vague or secretive eating patterns
- Blames failure in social and professional community on weight
- Weight gain
- Mood swings, depression, fatigue
- Insomnia, poor sleeping habits

Resources

Remuda Ranch Treatment Center
Remuda Ranch is located in Arizona, USA, and has a highly flexible and individualized program to meet each individual's exact needs regarding length of stay and level of care. It also has a website with amazing information on eating disorders and treatment. I highly recommend the articles written on anorexia, bulimia, and other eating disorders. There are also several articles written for parents of children with eating disorders and a great section on medical complications. Visit www.remudaranch.com.

Westwind Eating Disorder Recovery Centre
This recovery center is located in Manitoba, Canada. It is a collaborative treatment program for women. They work on goals with the individual rather than insisting on compliance to a set of rules. It also has a great website and blog on eating disorders. The blog keeps the readers involved and updated on new activities taking place at Westwind. There is also a Support Forum for both daughters and parents to post discussions, ask questions, and share thoughts. Included in this website is a section known as the "Dangers of Eating Disorders." Visit www.westwind.mb.ca.

Eating Recovery Center
This recovery center is located in Colorado, USA. It is the only center in the Rocky Mountain region that offers a full spectrum of eating recovery treatment options for male and female adults, adolescents, and children. Services offered include inpatient, residential, partial hospitalization, and outpatient programs—all of which are tailored to meet each individual patient's unique needs. Visit http://www.eatingrecoverycenter.com.

Woodstone Treatment Facility
This treatment facility is located in Galiano Island in British Columbia, Canada. This facility provides multidisciplinary specialized care for young people suffering from anorexia nervosa, bulimia nervosa, or eating disorders not otherwise specified. It is affiliated with the Looking Glass Foundation. Visit www.woodstoneresidence.org.

Looking Glass Foundation
The Looking Glass Foundation was developed by parents and friends who know the fear of living with a child with an eating disorder. There are plenty of resources, helpful links, and information regarding support groups for both the family and the child with the eating disorder. There is also a section called "Ask an Expert" in which you can ask the registered psychologist questions and receive an e-mail reply. Visit www.lookingglassbc.com.

Something Fishy
Something Fishy provides professional information and articles related to eating disorders. This site has an excellent section on what signs and symptoms to be aware of in identifying an eating disorder, what medications may be helpful for treatment, and what important blood and lab work tests should be done on a regular basis. Visit www.something-fishy.org.

There is also a questionnaire on this website that can be completed online, printed, and brought to the doctor for review. It is recommended for anyone who thinks they may have an eating disorder or can be completed by someone who knows someone who may have an eating disorder. Visit www/something-fishy.org/isf/questionnaire.php.

National Eating Disorders Association (NEDA)
NEDA is a world-renowned American association with a great website for families and educators. This website provides information on the causes of eating disorders, lists of helpful resources, stories of

hope, and valuable tips on how friends and family can offer support. Visit www.nationaleatingdisorders.org.

I highly recommend downloading the NEDA Parent Toolkit, as it offers information on a variety of issues in regards to eating disorders. Visit http://www.nationaleatingdisorders.org/information-resources/parent-toolkit.php.

Mirror Mirror

Mirror Mirror offers a wide array of information on eating disorders and treatments. I highly recommend the "Myths and Realities" section, as it dispels untruths and provides accurate information about eating disorders. Also, the Web page on "Additional Information" is helpful as it discusses other issues related to eating disorders, such as abuse, self injury, and addictions. Visit www.mirror-mirror.org.

Eating Disorders Helping Moms

This website provides information to support mothers of daughters with eating disorders. There is an article section that provides comprehensive information on the stages of eating disorders, including signs and symptoms. It also includes personal true stories written by family members. Visit www.eatingdisorders-helpingmoms.com.